JULIAN
Woman of our Day

Julian is not only a great lady of the past; she is also a great woman in our future. What Thomas Merton was to spirituality in the 1960s and 1970s, Julian of Norwich will be to the 1980s and 1990s.

(Herbert O'Driscoll in *The Mystics Quarterly*)

JULIAN

Woman of our Day

EDITED BY
Robert Llewelyn

TWENTY-THIRD PUBLICATIONS
Mystic, Connecticut

Third printing   October 1988

North American Edition 1987
Twenty-Third Publications
185 Willow Street
P.O. Box 180
Mystic, CT 06355
(203) 536-2611

First published in 1985 by
Darton, Longman and Todd Ltd.
89 Lillie Road
London SW6 1UD England

ISBN 0-89622-334-5
Library of Congress Catalog Card Number 86-51636

Cover design by Michael Harvey, based on a picture of
Julian of Norwich by Anna Dimascio.

Contents

Notes on Contributors

A. M. Allchin is a residentiary Canon of Canterbury Cathedral and Warden of the Sisters of the Love of God of Fairacres, Oxford. He is the author of several books of which the most recent is *The Joy of All Creation* (DLT 1984, published in USA by Cowley Press). He is at present working on a book on the doctrine of deification in Anglican tradition to be called *Participation in God*. His article first appeared in *The Medieval Mystical Tradition in England*, ed. Marion Glasscoe (University of Exeter 1980).

Sister Ritamary Bradley SFCC, member of the Sisters for Christian Community, is professor of English at St Ambrose College, Davenport, Iowa, USA. She is co-editor of *Mystics Quarterly* (University of Iowa) and has published and lectured extensively on medieval studies and especially on Julian. Her article first appeared in *Peaceweavers*, *Medieval Religious Women* II, Cistercian Series Studies 72, eds. Lillian Thomas Shank and John A. Nichols (Kalamazoo, Mich. 1985).

Richard Harries, formerly vicar of All Saints, Fulham, is Dean of King's College, London, and the author of ten books including *Being a Christian* (Mowbrays 1981, published in USA by Winston Press as *What Christians Believe*), *Prayer and the Pursuit of Happiness* (Collins 1985, published in USA by Eerdmans), and (with George Every and Kallistos Ware) *Seasons of the Spirit* (SPCK 1984, published in USA by St Vladimir's Seminary Press as *The Time of the Spirit*). He is widely known as a broadcaster and a number of his radio talks have been published including *Morning has Broken* (Marshall Pickering 1985).

Kenneth Leech, a priest who has served several London parishes, is Race Relations Field Officer of the Church of England Board for Social Responsibility. He is author of *Soul Friend* (1977), *True Prayer* (1980), *The Social God* (1981), and *True God* (1985), all published by Sheldon Press. The first two books and the last are published by Harper and Row in USA, the last under the title *Experiencing God*. His paper was originally given at the annual festival of the Order of Julian of Norwich at the Church of the Resurrection, Norwich, Connecticut, 11 May 1985.

Robert Llewelyn is Chaplain of the Julian Shrine in Norwich. He is author of *With Pity not with Blame* (DLT 1982) and *Love Bade Me Welcome* (DLT 1984) and general editor of the DLT 'Enfolded in Love' series. The first two books are published by Paulist Press in USA, the first under the title *All Shall Be Well – The Spirituality of Julian of Norwich for Today*.

Michael McLean is rector of Parmentergate, Norwich, where St Julian's is one of the parish churches, and an Honorary Canon of Norwich Cathedral. A member of General Synod for twelve years he was involved in the inclusion of Julian in the new Calendar. He instituted the annual Julian Lecture at the Shrine and has written a number of articles on associated subjects including a brief popular pamphlet *Who was Julian? A Beginner's Guide*.

Sister Elizabeth Ruth Obbard ODC is Novice Mistress at Walsingham Carmel. She is author of *Magnificat* (DLT 1985) and editor of *Lamps of Fire* (DLT 1985) in the 'Enfolded in Love' series. She is at present working on an introduction to the eremitical rule of St Albert.

Sister Anna Maria Reynolds CP has been a student of Julian's writings for over thirty years and has written several articles on Julian. Her partially modernized version of the Short Text of the *Revelations* from British Museum ms. 37790 (Longman 1956, reprinted Sheed and Ward 1974) has been translated into French and German. Sister Reynolds is at present on the staff of a retreat Centre of her Congregation at Drumalis, Larne, Co Antrim, Northern Ireland. Her article is a revised and expanded version of a paper originally printed in *Mystics Quarterly*, September 1984.

Father John Swanson OJN, an Episcopal priest in the USA, is Founder and Guardian of the Order of Julian of Norwich in Norwich, Connecticut. He is editor of the periodical papers, *Julian Jottings*, and currently has two works in progress on the contemplative life: *Tales of the Golden Castle* and *Wandering in God*.

Anna Dimascio, our cover artist, is a member of the Julian Shrine. She is interested in ecclesiastical design and especially icon painting. Her Julian and other icons are on sale at the Julian Shrine. Commissions for other work are accepted.

Acknowledgements

Thanks are due to Paulist Press for permission to quote from Edmund Colledge and James Walsh's translation of the *Revelations of Divine Love* and to Penguin Books for permission to quote from the translation by Clifton Wolters.

Preface

The late Bishop John Robinson has described Julian's theology as 'astonishingly whole and extraordinarily modern'. It is a remarkable tribute from a modern theologian to the writings of an obscure and 'unlettered' woman of six centuries ago. The *Revelations of Divine Love* – written first in a brief text of less than 20,000 words and later expanded four fold – is increasingly gaining the attention of informed men and women throughout the Church today. Julian has been described by Thomas Merton as a 'true theologian', meaning thereby that she perceived God truly, that her vision of the nature of his love corresponded with the reality itself.

In this book eight of us have come together – or nine with the writer of the introduction – to present one or another aspect of Julian's teaching. It is sent out from the Julian Shrine where, over a period of twenty years, Julian's own writing took shape, and I have the pleasant task of thanking the contributors for placing their writings at our disposal and generously donating their royalties to the developing work of the Shrine. In particular I would like to thank Michael McLean who, in the writing of the introduction, has undertaken the most difficult task in a book of this type, that of combining his own evaluation of Julian's teaching with insights expressed through the contributions of others.

Whilst each contributor deals with a different aspect of Julian's thought the reader will notice a small amount of overlapping. It could hardly be otherwise in a collection of this nature and I do not think it will be found tedious; indeed for those not well acquainted with Julian there may, perhaps, be some gain. At any rate I have felt that to prune at such points would weaken and perhaps in some measure destroy the integrity of the individual essay. Contributors have, too, been left free to select the translation of their choice. Their notes indicate the source from which the quotations are drawn.

Here in Julian's own city the work of the Shrine goes on. Her cell, pulled down at the Reformation, was rebuilt in 1952 on the site where it formerly stood. The work was undertaken largely through the initiative of the Community of All Hallows, Ditchingham, whose association with the parish goes back for over a hundred years. It now occupies perhaps twice the space of the original and is furnished as a chapel to which pilgrims come from all over the world to remain quietly in prayer. Those who wish to make an extended visit may stay at All Hallows (convent) guest-house next door to the church. Requests for prayer left by visitors or reaching us through the post are offered regularly at the Eucharist or in silent intercession. A well-stocked library adjoins the church and acts, too, as a meeting-place where problems may be shared and counsel given. The work is still very much in the making and we hope in time to provide better facilities for our flow of guests. The 'Friends of St Julian's'* has recently come into being whereby members hold us regularly in their prayers as we hold them. We trust, too, we may have the same bond between ourselves and our readers.

ROBERT LLEWELYN
The Julian Shrine
c/o All Hallows
Rouen Road
Norwich NR1 1QT

* Those who would like to know more are invited to write to The Secretary, Friends of St Julian's, 10 Norman's Buildings, Rouen Road, Norwich, NR1 1QT.

Introduction

Michael McLean

When the *Revelations of Divine Love* appeared in Grace Warrack's translation at the beginning of this century few people had even heard of Julian. Today she is the most widely read and influential mystic of the English spiritual tradition, the encourager and consoler of thousands of people throughout the world.

The anniversary of her 'shewings' on 8 May 1373 has been observed for many decades at the little church in Norwich where she lived and from which she took her name. But now visitors and pilgrims come throughout the year from countries everywhere. The accessibility of her writings through many recent translations, local and international scholarship, the impetus given by the 600th anniversary celebrations (at the initiative of Dean Alan Webster and the then Rector Charles Seear), her inclusion in the Calendar of the Alternative Service Book, and her growing reputation as a spiritual guide, draw thousands to her cell. In 1978 an annual lecture was instituted as a regular part of the yearly celebrations so that the Shrine might make a serious contribution to Julian studies.

Leading experts – including one from France and one from America – have delivered these lectures. Among them should be mentioned the late Bishop John Robinson whose perceptive contribution is published by the Shrine as 'A Woman for all Seasons' and now forms part of his book *The Roots of a Radical*.

The original intention for this present volume was to publish a collection of these lectures. Three of them, indeed, are included – those by Richard Harries, Dean of King's College London, Sister Anna Maria Reynolds, an eminent authority on the text of the *Revelations,* and John Swanson, founder of the Order of Julian of Norwich in America. But as the book has developed they have been augmented by five other essays. A. M. Allchin, of Canterbury, writes on Julian and The Tradition; Robert Llewelyn, Chaplain at the Shrine, on one aspect of Julian's theology; Sister Ritamary Bradley SFCC on Julian's prayer; Sister Elizabeth Ruth ODC on Julian and Teresa of Avila; and Kenneth Leech on contemplation and action. Some widen and deepen our theological understanding, some may well alter the style and quality of our Christian response to God's initiative, and Sister Ritamary's perceptive and profound analysis of the development of Julian's prayer may well help our own spiritual life. It is hoped that all of them will lead many people into a greater appreciation of Julian's significance for our generation.

For, as our title makes clear, we believe that Julian is a woman of our day; that in some mysterious providence of God her wisdom has been 'saved up' for our generation. In her lifetime she was clearly prepared to wait in patience. She waited for her youthful prayer for 'three graces from God' to be answered, and she waited twenty years for the meaning of her experiences in 1373 to be revealed. It may well be that she has waited six centuries for a people who could receive her message. The marked similarities between her age and ours encourage us to feel that she is our contemporary. Certainly no society has had greater need of her sanity, assurance, courage, obedience and vision. Her words are discovered to have particular relevance to the spiritual condition and quest of many people today, both within and without the Church.

It is the wholeness of her theology and her realism about our human life which are so attractive. These are qualities which are witnessed to by all contributors to this volume. John Swanson, for instance, insists that Julian is not only a 'theologian of essences and origins', but also a 'great pastoral teacher'. Canon Allchin writes that 'the truth and sureness of the divine and eternal perceptions in her book are validated

2

by the way in which they are rooted in the heart of human life and experience'. Sister Anna Maria, in her study of 'hope', makes it quite clear that Julian is not writing about some abstract theological virtue, but about a severely practical attitude which deeply affects our thinking and life-style. Kenneth Leech in his brilliantly imaginative encounter of Julian and John Ball emphasizes the necessary and intimate connection of mystical vision and prophetic action. Robert Llewelyn's thesis, that basic to Julian's theology is her revelation that 'there is no wrath in God', makes it plain that such an understanding has profound repercussions on our attitude to God, to other people, to sin, to suffering, to our very selves.

'Mystical' experiences and writing can too easily be thought to have little to do with the humdrum lives of ordinary people. Or they may seem to offer an exciting and high-flown escape from the pain of our lives. Kenneth Leech underlines both these dangers in the opening part of his essay, and points us throughout to what he calls 'incarnational, materialistic spirituality'. Conrad Pepler issued a warning many years ago: 'in every period of human turbulence', he wrote, 'enthusiasm flared up for mystics and mysticism . . . not always altruistic or very devout. It is tainted with the desire to escape from the bitter realities of human existence into remote realms of pleasant dreams.' Only the most superficial reader of the *Revelations* could get away with this sort of escapism. Julian is too keenly aware of the pains and ambiguities of life, too firmly anchored in the love of God and obedience to his will, to allow any sort of romanticism. She insists that whatever experiences or insights God granted her were meant to help her to live more fully both here and in eternity, and, in turn, to help her fellow-Christians to achieve true humanity. This concern with conformity to the will of God, rather than just with spiritual consolation, is fundamental to the *Revelations*, and it is drawn out very fully in Sister Elizabeth Ruth's essay. As the scribe of the Sloane manuscript writes in his colophon, 'this revelation is exalted divinity and wisdom and therefore it cannot remain with him who is a slave to sin and the devil . . . I pray that this book may not come into the hands of any except those who wish to be his faithful lovers, and

3

those who will submit themselves to the faith of the Church and obey'; a traditional formula maybe, but one which Julian would surely approve.

It is ever the mark of the true mystic, clear in Christian tradition of both east and west (as Canon Allchin points out), and thoroughly scriptural, that the vision of God necessarily involves and demands conversion. 'God of your goodness give me yourself', writes Julian, 'only in you do I have all'; and that 'all', as again Canon Allchin writes, 'contains all creation, given back to man by God, full of his energies of creation and redemption'. The mystic is the most practical of persons. Indeed it has been written 'the greatest problem of the world today is not air-pollution, nor population-explosion, nor sexual revolution, nor cultural change. The greatest problem . . . is our lack of mysticism. And the people who carry forward the thrust of evolution are the mystics. They are the vanguard, ecstatically pointing towards the future'.[1] Julian is one of those concerned with the future – man's fulfilment in God.

This fulfilment is through God's mercy and grace. The divine love yearns over man. This is the quality Sister Rita-mary describes so vividly as the thirst of God himself that he should have all humanity within himself. And the divine love, as revealed to Julian, centres on the passion of Christ, that most typical and complete manifestation of God's com-passion working to achieve man's true destiny. And God does this not from outside, but within man's abject condition. The incarnate Lord who suffers on the cross is the new Adam, not just in the sense that in him is a new creation, but that in him God shares in the first Adam's fall: 'the divinity rushed from the Father into the maiden's womb, falling to accept our nature'.[2] 'Adam's old tunic, tight-fitting, threadbare and short, was then made lovely by our Saviour, new, white and bright'.[3] Thus Julian sees that there is no part of man untouched by God – even that part which man in his blindness thinks unacceptable to God. St Paul writes, 'He hath made him to be sin for us, who knew no sin',[4] and Julian, 'He who is highest and most honourable was most foully brought low, most utterly despised'.[5]

4

God does this, according to Julian, because he 'wants us to understand and to believe that we are more truly in heaven than on earth'.[6] 'For I saw very surely that our substance is in God, and I also saw that God is in our sensuality, for in the same instant and place in which our soul is made sensual, in that same instant and place exists the city of God';[7] and 'when our soul is breathed into our body, at which time we are made sensual, at once mercy and grace begin to work . . . in which operation the Holy Spirit forms in our faith the hope that we shall return up above to our substance'.[8]

So, as John Swanson writes: 'Salvation is found in our true created natures; salvation is a restoration not an innovation – a return to our true and original participation in the Holy Trinity . . . we are perfectible *because* of our nature, not in *spite* of our nature. To be a full and complete person is to be in union with God.'

This is teaching of great joy, great liberation. All that we are, even our 'lower' part – that created being of this earthly life which Julian calls our 'sensuality' – is totally acceptable, loved and redeemed. 'God is everything that is good . . . and God has made everything that is made, and God loves everything he has made.'[9]

This is a far cry from that manichaeism which is so persistent – and so destructive – in the life of the Church, right up to the present day. Julian is thoroughly orthodox in revealing a fuller understanding of man's created, redeemed, and future glory. She is sure that love, who creates all things, will bring all things to perfection.

> We shall by his sweet grace . . . come into him now in this present life. And then [in heaven] we shall come into our Lord, knowing ourselves clearly, and wholly possessing God . . . truly seeing, and wholly feeling, and hearing him spiritually, and delectably smelling him, and sweetly tasting him. And there we shall see God face to face, familiarly and wholly.[10]

It is clear from this that Julian's eschatology is at once 'realized' and 'future'. Already our 'substance' is in God, and by redemptive grace our sensuality is being raised to its level.

This will be completed in the vision of God. Such an understanding of redemption goes far beyond common thoughts of
life-after-death. It is a similar sort of understanding to that
which the doctrine of the Assumption of the Blessed Virgin
seeks to express (a theological rather than an historic 'event')
– that by God's grace all that man is, body, mind, spirit, is
somehow to be taken into divinity. 'Christ the first-fruit,
afterwards they that are Christ's.'[11]

Julian's thought is thoroughly Pauline; indeed she appears
to be soaked in his writings – particularly the letter to the
Romans. Like him, Julian understands that redemption is
concerned not just with humankind but with the whole
creation which 'retains the hope of being freed, like us, from
its slavery to decadence, to enjoy the same freedom ·as the
children of God'.[12] Her cosmic, 'nuclear' vision of 'a small
thing, no bigger than a hazelnut' (ch. 5) taught her that
everything has being through the love of God, he loves it and
preserves it. And if such a tiny insignificant thing, which
would fall into dust without this amazing and sustaining love,
is of infinite value, then indeed *all* things must be well. Such
assurance is not some kind of human optimism, but a
consciousness of God's total power.

Again Julian is following St Paul in recognizing that the
redemption is concerned with mankind in its entirety. Just as
there is a solidarity between Christ and his people, so there
is solidarity between each member and the other: '[he] will
draw our outer disposition to the inward, and will make us
all at unity with him, and each of us with others in the true
lasting joy which is Jesus';[13] or, again, 'in the sight of God
all men are one man, and one man is all men'.[14]

This is an aspect of Julian's teaching brought out forcibly
by Kenneth Leech, Richard Harries, and Sister Anna Maria,
in their essays. It is basic to Julian, for she sees at once
the infinite value of each individual soul and the unity of
humankind: 'If I pay special attention to myself, I am
nothing; but in general I am, I hope, in the unity of love with
all my fellow-Christians. For it is in this unity that the life of
all men consists who will be saved.'[15]

Julian receives in her showings, and in her meditations

upon them, image after image which attempt to describe the
infinity and completeness of God's love. It is overwhelming;
beyond our imagining. Her famous image of the motherhood
of God (which seems to speak so vividly to our generation –
perhaps in correction of our over-masculine ideas and social
structures – and which has done much to rid us of false
concepts of the angry, unapproachable, patriarchal God) is
but one example of her attempts. The totality of love is so
great that, as Richard Harries writes, 'every aspect of [her]
thought has the seeds of universalism in it'. She is too loyal
a daughter of the Church to go beyond the limits of orthodoxy;
and indeed constantly professes her submission to the doctrine
of Holy Church. But, while she lived in a Church which
appears to have been somewhat obsessed with 'damnation'
(pictures of the Doom decorating every chancel arch), she
is certainly willing to stand uncomfortably on the brink of
heterodoxy. She faces honestly the apparently irreconcilable
paradox that, on one hand, God 'shall make all well that is
not well', and, on the other, that his love is such that those
who choose some self-inflicted hell must be free to be there.
She stands firm in faith before such dilemmas, assured by
God that what is impossible for man is possible for God.
And she reconciles the dilemma for herself by accepting the
revelation that God will do a 'great deed' – a deed at present
unknowable to man: 'There is a deed which the Blessed
Trinity will perform on the last day, as I see it, and what the
deed will be and how it will be performed is unknown to
every creature . . . and will be until the deed is done.'[16]

Such a faithful agnosticism is almost inevitable in one who
has so great a sense of the power and glory of God. Although
'God is closer to us than our own soul, for he is the foundation
in which our soul stands',[17] yet 'we do not keep our promise
or the purity which God has established in us, but often fall
back into so much wretchedness that it is shameful to say
it';[18] 'we fall back into ourselves, through depression and
spiritual blindness'.[19] Fallen people, as we all are, cannot
know the hidden mercies and meaning of God to the full.
Our faces may be turned towards the sun, but we cannot

open our eyes to look upon it; indeed, were we to do so now, we would be blinded.

For Julian certainly has a realistic understanding of our sin and frailty. She in no way glosses over our betrayal of true humanity and the will of God. She herself knew vascillation between delight and despair: 'in the time of joy I could have said with St Paul, "nothing shall separate me from the love of Christ", and in the pain I could have said with St Peter, "Lord save me, I am perishing" '.[20] She was oppressed, weary, abandoned to herself, filled with a sense of her own wretchedness. She felt her cell to be a prison. She knew bewilderment, despair, doubts about her own sanity, scepticism about the authenticity of what she had received from God, violent attacks from the devil. The main thrust of her writing may, as has been said, 'start from the sun, not the clouds', but she is painfully aware of the darkness. Indeed for Julian, as for all who have experienced something of the glory of God, the darkness is heightened by the radiance of the sun. Though she found the darkness to be light enough, yet it was no easier for her, than for any of us, to be faithful to the vision. 'Our Lord gave me to understand that the vision would pass, and it is faith which preserves the blessed revelation through grace.'[21]

It is this faith which enables her to accept that whatever happens, all things – even the painful ones – indeed particularly the painful ones since they are a means of identity with the passionate Christ – work together for good for those who love God: 'he did not say, "you will not be assailed, you will not be belaboured, you will not be disquieted", but he did say, "you will not be overcome" '.[22]

Even sin itself, that 'sharpest scourge . . . which belabours and breaks a man',[23] purges him and turns bitterness, by contrition, into hope of God's mercy. Shame is turned into honour and glory. So sin is behovely. In some strange mercy of God it is used for his purposes in the restoration of man to true humanity. Julian remains baffled by this mystery, but she is led to believe that we shall ultimately comprehend.[24]

She understands too that sin has no being of itself; it is nothing for it is no part of God's creating. It is absence of true humanity, as John Swanson makes clear. However dreadful, it cannot prevent God's goodness from working. What is more God looks on his servant 'with pity not with blame',[25] and, more amazingly, 'we do not fall in the sight of God'[26] even though 'we do not stand in our own sight'.[27] God is total love, and what we experience as punishment from God – that wrath within, which is entirely of our own making – is nothing else than the love of God who 'waits for us continually, mourning and moaning until we come'.[28]

In his study of the constancy and consolation of God's love Robert Llewelyn draws out the implications for our lives of such an understanding – and Julian herself states clearly that the Lord revealed his meaning to her because he wishes to have it better known that it is. 'He longs to teach us to know him and to love him always more and more . . . he longs to bring us up to bliss.'[29]

It is so that this joyful message, given through Julian so many centuries ago, might be better understood today, as she wished, that these essays have been written. May they help us all to penetrate more fully into the revelations she received, and, as she begged us, to contemplate Jesus who is teacher of all.

1 William Johnston sj, *Silent Music* (London 1976), p. 165.
2 *Revelations of Divine Love* ch. 51. I have used the translation by E. Colledge and J. Walsh (London and New York 1978).
3 ibid.
4 2 Cor. 5:21.
5 *RDL* ch. 20.
6 *RDL* ch. 55.
7 ibid.
8 ibid.
9 *RDL* ch. 9.
10 *RDL* ch. 43.
11 1 Cor. 15:23.
12 Rom. 8:21.
13 *RDL* ch. 71.
14 *RDL* ch. 51.
15 *RDL* ch. 9.
16 *RDL* ch. 32.
17 *RDL* ch. 56.

18 *RDL* ch. 73.
19 *RDL* ch. 64.
20 *RDL* ch. 15.
21 *RDL* ch. 70.
22 *RDL* ch. 68.
23 *RDL* ch. 39.
24 *RDL* ch. 27 *passim.*
25 *RDL* ch. 82.
26 ibid.
27 ibid.
28 *RDL* ch. 79.
29 *RDL* ch. 75.

Woman of Hope

Anna Maria Reynolds CP

In a brilliant opening chapter to his book *Hope is the Remedy*, Bernard Häring depicts a 'Universal Congress of Skunks', presided over by the Supervisor of Devils, the Super-Skunk. The main item on its agenda is to formulate 'a new unified strategy the goal of which is nothing less than the transformation of the Church, our enemy, into a perfect sacrament of pessimism, a truly visible and effective sign of our infernal odour'.[1] According to the advice of Super-Skunk, they can let Christians get away with anything provided they destroy hope and inject pessimism. Christian living cannot long survive without hope, he points out, so to destroy hope is to ensure victory for the Devils.

In this context, presented as a serious threat to Christian living in today's world, I think it may be profitable to explore what Julian of Norwich, so experienced in discerning the wiles of the Evil One, has to offer by way of a counter-strategy.

Most students of the *Revelations* are struck by Julian's optimism. This is not surprising, since optimism is a quality that pervades her writings. What is surprising, however, is the fact that most of the time we take this aspect of Julian's book for granted. We think of England in the fourteenth century as 'merry England', a land full of colour, song, gaiety, dance and enjoyment, as the historians tell us it was.[2] But we tend to ignore the dark side of medieval life, also testified to by the historians: the prevalence of disease, the savage and vindictive punishments which could mean having a hand or foot struck off for theft, or allow an offender to be blinded or mutilated; the cheapness of human life, such that a historian could write

11

with conviction: 'If the conditions of the Middle Ages were reproduced for a week or two in modern times the newspapers would have reason for their alarm.'[3]

The close of the Middle Ages was, in fact, throughout Europe a period of violence, cruelty and pessimism. J. Huisinga declares:

> Calamities and indigence were more afflicting than at present; it was more difficult to guard against them and to find solace. Illness and health presented a more striking contrast . . . Honours and riches were relished with greater avidity and contrasted more vividly with surrounding misery.[4]

> All things presenting themselves to the mind in violent contrasts and impressive forms, lent a tone of excitement and of passion to everyday life and tended to produce that perpetual oscillation between despair and distracted joy, between cruelty and pious tenderness, which characterizes life in the Middle Ages.[5]

It is not astonishing that life in such an unstable and violent world should be more inclined to pessimism than to optimism, and so we read:

> At the close of the Middle Ages, a sombre melancholy weighs on people's souls. Whether we read a chronicle, a poem, a sermon, a legal document even, the same impression of immense sadness is produced by them all. It would sometimes seem as if this period had been particularly unhappy, as if it had left behind only the memory of violence, of covetousness and mortal hatred, as if it had known no other enjoyment but that of intemperance, of pride and of cruelty.[6]

Closely allied with this melancholy was a view of death as something gruesome and dismal, culminating in the macabre idea of the 'dance of death'. Indeed, the dominant thought about death as expressed in the literature, both ecclesiastical and lay, of this period, knows but two extremes: the brevity of earthly glory, and jubilation over the salvation of the soul.

All else is overshadowed by the over-accentuated and over-vivid representation of death as hideous and threatening – a horrid image of skeletons and worms.

Such are the characteristics of the epoch to which Julian belongs and which projects her as a radiant figure of pure goodness vibrant with faith, hope and love. The source of the optimism and serenity which Julian diffuses is neither biological – a matter of temperament – nor physical – a matter of feeling good and comfortable in an unchallenging situation, since her situation was, in fact, a desperately challenging one. She repeatedly makes clear that her cheerfulness rests on something outside herself:

> The remedy is that our Lord is with us, keeping us and leading us into the fullness of joy; for our Lord intends this to be an endless joy, that he who will be our bliss when we are there [in heaven] is our protector while we are here, our way and our heaven in true love and trust.[7]

This quotation is taken from near the end of Julian's book where she is reiterating the need for total trust in, and dependence on, God's infinitely tender and compassionate love for even the most feeble and wretched of his children. The theme was, however, presented at the beginning of the book when Julian was giving an account of the first showing. In that account she mentions three truths which focus and give significance to all her subsequent reflections. They are: God's love as expressed in the passion of Christ; God's love as expressed in his creation and providence; and the response which God's love should evoke in the creature.

The first revelation granted to Julian was a showing of the crowning of Christ 'as it were in the time when the crown of thorns was pressed on his blessed head. I perceived, truly and powerfully, that it was he who just so, both God and man, himself suffered for me'.[8] Suddenly the Trinity filled her heart with joy for she understood that because of the passion of the God-man 'there was strength enough for me and indeed for every living creature, against every fiend of hell and all temptations'.[9] This is the first truth. It contains a guarantee of victory for the soul of good will no matter what the odds

13

against it. Trials and temptations there may be in abundance, but defeat, never.

The second truth is conveyed through the showing of the hazelnut: 'something small, no bigger than a hazelnut, lying in the palm of my hand, as it seemed to me, and it was as round as a ball'.[10] Julian wonders what it is and is told interiorly: ' "It is all that is made." ' While she is expecting the object to disintegrate, it was so small, she is again answered in her mind: 'It lasts and always will, because God loves it; and thus everything has being through the love of God.'[11] From this showing Julian learns two lessons, both of them important for her growth in hope. First, she is helped to appreciate the power and awesomeness of the Creator, in whose presence the entire created universe appears of no more significance than a hazelnut held in the palm of one's hand; and secondly, she learns that, insignificant though it may appear, God loves and cares for it. He is not only the maker, but the keeper and the lover. Furthermore, she is made aware that, if this holds good of things, it is incredibly more true of God's love and care for his children.

The third truth, that God expects from his creatures a response of loving obedience and trustful dependence, is brought out in the showing of our Lady:

> God showed me part of the wisdom and the truth of her soul, and in this I understood the reverent contemplation with which she beheld her God, who is her Creator, marvelling with great reverence that he was willing to be born of her who was a simple creature created by him. And this wisdom and truth, this knowledge of her Creator's greatness and of her own created littleness, made her say very meekly to Gabriel: 'Behold me here, God's handmaiden'.[12]

In this way the strength and foundation of Julian's whole lesson of love and hope were revealed in the first showing. The theme is orchestrated in the subsequent showings and the remaining eighty or so chapters of the *Revelations*.

But before looking more closely at Julian's writings it will be helpful to clarify the concept of 'hope' in general and of 'Christian hope' in particular. According to Rahner:

Hope is not simply the attitude of one who is weak and at the same time hungering for a fulfilment, but rather the courage *to commit oneself in thought and deed to the incomprehensible and uncontrollable which permeates our existence* (i.e. God) and, as the future to which it is open, sustains it.[13]

Hope, then, is a capacity to rely totally on another to achieve for us what we are unable to achieve by our own efforts. *Christian* hope is motivated by an unshakeable belief in a God the Father who loves us, in his Son who saves and frees us, in the Spirit who directs us. It abides in such basic objects as God's personal love for each of us; his willingness to forgive each of us over and over again; his giving constantly to each one of us new strength because of our weakness; his freeing us from all that could hamper our drawing closer to him each day; and, finally, in his overruling providence which lovingly controls the entire universe.[14] Christian hope is a gift. But a gift has to be accepted if it is to become operative in our lives. As Häring puts it:

Christ is our hope through faith, but faith conceived as an absolute readiness to listen to him, to treasure up his words in our heart, meditating and acting upon them. It is faith understood as a joyous, grateful acceptance of the one who is our Saviour, our hope.[15]

I shall attempt to demonstrate that Julian's writings, looked at in the light of the definitions given above, portray the anchoress as a woman animated by a mature and profound Christian hope.

Julian's hope is challenged by her acute awareness of two unpleasant facts – her own sinfulness and the presence of sin, evil and suffering in the world she lived in. Awareness of her own sinfulness causes her to say:

Sin is the sharpest scourge with which any chosen soul can be struck, which scourge belabours man or woman, and breaks a man, and purges him in his own sight so much that at times he thinks himself that he is not fit for anything but as it were to sink into hell . . .[16]

15

> And this is a supreme friendship of our courteous Lord, that he protects us so tenderly whilst we are in our sins . . . But when we see ourselves so foul, then we believe that God may be angry with us because of our sins.[17]

> For sin is so vile and so much to be hated that it can be compared to no pain which is not sin. And no more cruel hell than sin was revealed to me, for a loving soul hates no pain but sin . . .[18]

Julian knows full well that, when repented of, sin is forgiven and forgotten by God, yet she is tormented by an attempt to reconcile in her own mind two apparently irreconcilable truths, namely, that we are all sinners and yet God does not blame us. Her longing to see a way out of this problem persisted and, at last, she says: 'our courteous Lord answered very mysteriously, by revealing a wonderful example of a lord who has a servant, and gave me sight for the understanding of both'.[19]

Briefly, the parable of the lord and the servant depicts a servant sent on an errand by his master; in his eagerness to fulfil his master's behest the servant stumbles, falls, and is unable to proceed on his errand despite his desire to do so. In his distress he cannot bear even to look at his lord so he does not know how he has taken his servant's failure.

The interpretation of the parable is long and complex, incorporating insights received in the course of years of pondering its significance. One thing Julian is taught clearly, however, is that the relationship between God and man is not broken by human failure. The servant falls and experiences confusion, distress and sorrow because of his fall; indeed, he is so concerned about it that he is unaware of the compassion and love with which his lord was regarding him and so fails to realize that no blame is being imputed to him, the servant, by his master. In the same way, Julian suggests, God is more anxious to reward sinners for the pain of their falling than to punish them for having fallen. In her detailed explanation of the meaning of the parable Julian underlines for us the truth that Jesus is the visible manifestation of the divinity to man as well as the chief representative of man before God; that he

16

is not only the second person of the Trinity but also the head
of the body of Christ:

> For the longing and desire of all mankind which shall be
> saved appeared in Jesus, for Jesus is in all who will be
> saved, and all who will be saved are in Jesus, *and all is of
> the love of God*, with obedience, meekness and patience, and
> the virtues which befit us.[20]

Because Christ has taken upon himself all our 'blame' and
we are members of his body, the Father, explains Julian, may
not and does not wish to assign more blame to us than to his
own beloved Son, Jesus Christ; and her detailed interpretation
of the parable ends with a picture of Christ sitting in triumph
at his Father's right hand in heaven, 'in rest and in peace',
with redeemed mankind symbolized by a 'rich and precious
crown' upon his head. And so her problem about sin and
'blame' is laid to rest. Her experiencing of the parable enabled
her to look beyond the creature's weakness and inadequate
efforts to the compassionate and supportive love of God. And
this reliance on the sight of God's love in its turn generated
a vision of strength and fresh hope. God loves us because *he*
is good, not because *we* are good.

The second major challenge to Julian's hope is the presence
in the world of evil and suffering. Just as she had wondered
why God had not prevented sin, so she mused with anxiety
on why he permitted

> all which is not good, and the shameful contempt and the
> direst tribulation which he endured for us in this life, and
> his death and all his pains, and the passions, spiritual and
> bodily, of all his creatures.[21]

Our Lord's immediate answer to her unease is: 'Sin is
necessary, but all shall be well and all shall be well and all
manner of thing shall be well.'[22] And Julian comments:

> And in these same words I saw hidden in God an exalted
> and wonderful mystery, which he will make plain and we
> shall know in heaven. In this knowledge we shall truly see

17

the cause why he allowed sin [and evil] to come, and in this sight we shall rejoice forever.[23]

A modern scholar, Patricia Vinje, has some interesting and illuminating observations to offer on this passage:

It is particularly significant that Julian used this theme to deal with the element of the unknown. Whereas the bulk of Julian's teaching in the *Book of Showings* stresses the importance of knowing as much as one could about God's love, this theme honours the inevitable incomprehensibility of divine love. The realization that creatures cannot and ought not to know everything God has planned for them actually brings a sigh of tremendous relief.

Julian kept alive a hope that some great deed ordained by God would *make all thyng wele*. She had no inkling as to what would actually come to pass but this in itself did not trouble her. She stressed that Christ's followers did not need to know God's designs . . .[24]

Hidden behind this mild admonition to curb one's curiosity, Julian was planting the seeds of a firm theology of hope in the face of spiritual desolation and abandonment. She encouraged her followers to believe that everything is in God's hands when they do not have a clue as to what God is going to do next. In doing so she offered her fellow-Christians an example of how to abandon themselves to God in the midst of desolation and how to utterly trust God in all things, because he alone has the power to make all things well.[25]

Julian is, of course, aware that it can, at times, be extremely difficult to do just this, and she reflects regretfully:

And it is about this knowledge [of God's love] that we are most blind, for some of us believe that God is almighty and may do everything, and that he is all wisdom and can do everything, but that he is all love and will do everything – there we fail. And it is this ignorance that most hinders God's lovers, as I see it.[26]

Thanks to her personal experience of God's love through the showings she can now say with complete conviction:

> He did not say, 'You will not be troubled, you will not be hard pressed, you will not be disquieted'. But he said, 'You will not be overcome'. God wants us to pay attention to these words, and always to be strong in faithful trust, in weal and in woe, for he loves us and delights in us, ahd so he wills us to love him and delight in him and trust mightily in him, and *all shall be well*.[27]

On this very positive and hope-filled note the showings cease, for Julian adds: 'And soon all was hidden, and I saw no more after this.'[28]

As one would expect from what has been said up to this point, Julian's writings display the characteristics normally associated with authentic Christian hope. They assume acceptance by their readers of the basic doctrines of the Christian creed.[29] The motivation is biblical. It rests on scriptural concepts familiar to Julian from the teaching of the Church and experienced by her in her personal spiritual life: the rock-like dependability of God, all of whose deeds are perfect and all of whose ways are just; the Creator who knit us together in our mother's womb and to whom all our ways lie open; the God of the impossible; the God who is Father and Mother to his children; the God who is always near, whose right hand holds us fast; the God who is rich in mercy; the God who loves us and delivered himself up to death for us. Her hope rests on, and is nourished by, the truths enshrined in these concepts.

Despite her experience of her own weakness she is, therefore, ready to commit herself in thought and deed to the 'incomprehensible and incontrollable'.

> And so I understood that any man or woman who voluntarily chooses God in his lifetime, for love, he may be sure that he is endlessly loved with an endless love which makes that grace in him. For he wants us to pay true heed to this, that we are as certain in our hope to have the bliss of

19

heaven while we are here, as we shall be certain of it when we are there.[30]

Later, she makes explicit what is involved in 'choosing God':

> We are liable through our feebleness and folly to fall, and we are able through the mercy and grace of the Holy Spirit to rise to greater joy . . . So this is the remedy, that we acknowledge our wretchedness and flee to our Lord; for always, the more abased we are, the more profitable it is for us to touch him.[31]

For, as she had earlier explained: 'It is his [Christ's] office to save us, it is his glory to do it, and it is his will that we know it; for he wants us to love him sweetly and trust him meekly and mightily.'[32]

Julian's hope, moreover, is what Häring calls 'dialogical', that is, it can be understood only in terms of interpersonal relationship. Our relatedness to Christ, our whole life, can be response, but God's word must precede our reply. This is the case with Julian throughout the *Revelations*, from her first explicit response to 'the touch of the Holy Spirit':

> God of your goodness give me yourself, for you are enough for me, and I can ask nothing which is less that can pay you full worship. And if I ask anything which is less, always I am in want; but only in you do I have everything.[33]

The loving questioning of Christ in the ninth revelation, with Julian's glad reply, is another explicit example:

> 'Are you well satisified that I suffered for you?' I said: 'Yes, good Lord, all my thanks to you; yes, good Lord, blessed may you be.' Then Jesus our good Lord said: 'If you are satisfied, I am satisfied. It is a joy, a bliss, an endless delight to me that ever I suffered my Passion for you; and if I could suffer more, I would suffer more.'[34]

The parable of the lord and the servant and the chapters dealing with the theme 'God is our Mother' afford more extended examples of this dialogical aspect of Julian's hope.[35]

Furthermore, her hope exhibits the characteristic of *soli-*

darity in love emphasized in Paul's epistle to the Ephesians (4:1–16), and in the Vatican Council document *The Church in the Modern World*, articles 11 and 12. Speaking of her showings, Julian proclaims her solidarity with all her fellow-Christians:

> Everything I say about myself I mean to apply to all my fellow-Christians, for I am taught that this is what our Lord intends in this spiritual revelation . . . and you who hear and see this vision and this teaching . . . it is God's will and my wish that you accept it with as much joy and delight as if Jesus had shown it to you as he did to me . . . for it is common and general, just as we are all one.[36]

> . . . in general I am in the unity of love with all my fellow-Christians. For it is in this unity of love that the life consists of all men who will be saved.[37]

But such love must be active. The dynamism of hope is *faith active in love*. Love must be shown to friends and enemies alike; it must be expressed in gratitude, generosity, creativity and openness. Julian expresses her 'active love' not only in a general way by her life-style or 'vocation', but specifically by her prayer for all men, by her deep concern for her fellow-men good and bad, Christian or non-Christian, and by her willingness to share the spiritual riches with which she was graced.

Finally, Christian hope is joyful in character. As Häring remarks: 'From beginning to end, the Christian religion is one of promise, hope and fidelity.'[38] Julian's joyfulness is all-pervasive: 'She finds it necessary to discuss "joy" and "bliss" and their synonyms in no fewer than fifty-five different places in the *Revelations*, or at least once every three pages for the entire book.'[39] Her vision of the Lord is itself a vision of joy:

> And after this our Lord showed himself to me, and he appeared to me more glorified than I had seen him before, in which I was taught that our soul will never have rest till it comes to him, acknowledging that he is full of joy, familiar and courteous and blissful and true life.[40]

The joy of the Trinity is present in Christ:

21

For we know in our faith . . . that Jesus Christ is both God
and man; and in his divinity he is himself supreme bliss
and was from without beginning, and he will be without
end, which true ever-lasting bliss cannot of its nature be
increased or diminished.[41]

To know Christ, therefore, is to know joy. The movement of
the Trinity into the created order is the delight of the Trinity,
and the union of man with God creates joy in man, so that
our lives reflect the joy of the Trinity. Julian sees great significance in human joy; as a reflection of our relationship to the
Trinity we are meant to be full of joy and to know God in
his love, though, in fact, we can never appreciate the full
extent of God's love for us. In its fullness, this joy will be
experienced by all God's faithful ones who persevere in his
love:

And verily and truly, he will manifest to us all this marvellous joy when we shall see him . . . For the greatest abundance of joy which we shall have, as I see it, is this
wonderful courtesy and familiarity of our Father who is our
Creator, in our Lord Jesus Christ, who is our brother and
Saviour.[42]

Julian expands this aspect in a later chapter where she draws
a contrast between the spiritual man as he appears in this
life – weak, wretched and dependent – and his transformation
when he is brought up to heaven, where

it will truly be made known to us what he means in the
sweet words when he says: 'All shall be well, and you will
see it yourself, that every kind of thing shall be well.' And
then will the bliss of our motherhood in Christ begin anew
in the joys of our Father, God, which new beginning will
last, newly beginning, without end.[43]

This last quotation brings out another quality of Christian
hope frequently referred to in modern theology[44] – its eschato-
logical thrust:

With a gratitude based on God's fidelity, on everything he
has done, the Christian can look back knowing that God,

22

who has so wonderfully begun his work in creation, is pursuing it in an ineffable way in Jesus Christ, and will fulfil it in him on the day of the parousia.[45]

From the foregoing brief survey it is, I think, clear, that Julian was a woman in whom Christian hope was alive and active, based, not on her own virtuous performance but on the goodness, love and reliability of God as revealed in scripture and in the person of Christ. She was aware not only of her wretchedness and great need but also of the 'everlasting goodness' and 'blessed love' of God. Secure in this 'knowing', Julian is confident, serene, joyful and optimistic, so that she can conclude with calm certitude that:

> when the judgement is given, and we are all brought up above we shall then clearly see in God the mysteries which are now hidden from us. And then shall none of us be moved to say in any matter: 'Lord, if it had been so, it would have been well.' But we shall all say with one voice: 'Lord, blessed may you be, because it is so, it is well; and now we see truly that everything is done as it was ordained by you before anything was made.'[46]

By way of underlining my claim that Julian is indeed 'a woman of hope', I should like to quote once more from Patricia Vinje's book on the *Revelations*. She is concluding her section on England in Julian's day.

> The literature of this period reflects a spirit of pessimism brought on by the wars, sickness and the depressed economy. Julian of Norwich's writings provided an unhoped-for-relief from this contemporary strain of gloom. Julian shone as a herald of hope in the face of a social and religious depression. Her writings acknowledge the difficulties of life without succumbing to them. Like many of her contemporaries, she touched on the theme of agony and death and grief, but she managed to present these miseries within a vision of a better life, not only in heaven, but on this side of death. She urged her *even-Christians* to look beyond the immediate difficulties of life to future days and she encouraged them to cope with the present hard times by extending

compassion toward one another. Julian never erased the suffering of her people, but she did ennoble it.[47]

Her message of hope makes Julian, to my mind, supremely relevant to all of us living in today's fearful and threat-ridden world for it has been truly said that 'There is real danger at present of a Christianity without an *Alleluia*'.[48] All of us who are striving to lead a truly spiritual life must aim at restoring the *Alleluia* to Christianity; it is what the world expects from us as the following true story, sad but amusing, makes clear. Two Sisters were returning home one evening on a public bus. Tired and a little dejected after a tough day at school in a deprived area, they sat in solemn and unsmiling silence, oblivious of what was going on around them. After a few minutes a workman sitting opposite them could endure it no longer. He leaned over to his mate, and with a jerk of his thumb in the direction of the Sisters, said in a loud whisper, '*No wonder Jesus wept*'. History does not record the reaction of the Sisters, but let us hope that they managed to smile!

Häring emphasizes the obligation on Christians to be messengers of hope: 'What the world expects from the People of God is, above all, a realistic message of hope, the courage to be and to live in the midst of the pangs of childbirth with a hope that gives new life.'[49] Father John Dalrymple, well-known spiritual writer, makes the same point in the context of such 'gigantic and intractable' contemporary problems as the arms trade, multinational exploitation, racial discrimination, mass unemployment, Third World poverty and hunger.

> The distinctive contribution of Christians to the struggle for peace and justice has to be hope. A glance at the crucifix on the wall should always be sufficient to remind us that God is not defeated, in the long term, by the force of human selfishness, however much the short term prospect is 'hopeless'. Since the resurrection we have no need to run away from Gethsemane when the cause seems lost.[50]

Julian, in her *Revelations*, is conveying precisely the same message. Let us practise what she preaches.

References to the *Revelations* are to the modernized text by Edmund Colledge
and James Walsh, preface by Jean Leclercq (London and New York 1978).
I have, however, occasionally taken the liberty (without notice) of substi-
tuting my own translation for a word or phrase in the Colledge/Walsh
version.

1 Bernard Häring, *Hope is the Remedy* (Slough 1971), pp. 15–16.
2 L. F. Salzman, *English Life in the Middle Ages* (Oxford 1926, 1972), p. 24.
3 ibid. p. 10.
4 J. Huisinga, *The Waning of the Middle Ages* (New York 1954 edn), p. 9.
5 ibid. p. 10.
6 ibid. p. 31.
7 *RDL* ch. 77 p. 331.
8 *RDL* ch. 4, p. 181.
9 *RDL* ch. 4, p. 182.
10 *RDL* ch. 5, p. 183.
11 ibid.
12 *RDL* ch. 4, p. 182.
13 Gerald A. McCool (ed.), *A Rahner Reader* (London 1975), p. 239 (italics
mine).
14 Sister Marie Bela, 'Living as Women of Hope', *Sisters Today*, vol. 44,
no. 8 (April 1973), pp. 461–72 *passim*.
15 Häring, *Hope is the Remedy*, p. 23.
16 *RDL* ch. 39 p. 244.
17 *RDL* ch. 40, p. 246.
18 *RDL* ch. 40, p. 247.
19 *RDL* ch. 51, p. 267.
20 *RDL* ch. 51, p. 276.
21 *RDL* ch. 27, p. 225.
22 ibid.
23 *RDL* ch. 27, p. 226.
24 Patricia Mary Vinje, *An Understanding of Love According to the Anchoress
Julian of Norwich* (Salzburg 1983), p. 204.
25 ibid. p. 205.
26 *RDL* ch. 73, p. 323.
27 *RDL* ch. 68, p. 315.
28 ibid.
29 i.e. The Unity and Trinity of God, the incarnation, death and resurrection of the second person of the Trinity
30 *RDL* ch. 65, p. 308
31 *RDL* ch. 77, pp. 329–30.
32 *RDL* ch. 61, p. 302.
33 *RDL* ch. 5, p. 184.
34 *RDL* ch. 22, p. 216.
35 See *RDL* chs. 51 and 59–61 respectively.
36 *RDL*, Short Text, ch. 6, p. 134.

37 ibid.
38 Häring, *Hope is the Remedy*, p. 86.
39 Brant Pelphrey, *Love Was His Meaning: the theology and mysticism of Julian of Norwich* (Salzburg 1982), p. 143.
40 *RDL* ch. 26, p. 223.
41 *RDL* ch. 31, p. 230.
42 *RDL* ch. 7, p. 189.
43 *RDL* ch. 63, p. 305.
44 See, for example, J. Moltmann, *Theology of Hope* (New York 1976), pp. 291–303, and Häring, *Hope is the Remedy*, pp. 135–43.
45 Häring, *Hope is the Remedy*, p. 137.
46 *RDL* ch. 85, p. 341.
47 Vinje, *An Understanding of Love*, pp. 40–1.
48 Kevin O'Shea, *On Trial for Hope* (Melbourne 1970), p. 107.
49 Häring, *Hope is the Remedy*, p. 9.
50 John Dalrymple, *The Cross a Pasture* (London 1983), p. 77.

Julian of Norwich and the Continuity of Tradition

A. M. Allchin

We are living at a time when everywhere on our planet men and women are conscious of being confronted with enormous changes in their way of life, in their way of seeing the things around them and in their way of understanding and expressing what goes on inside them. It is a time when a great many traditions of every kind seem to be collapsing, when people's thoughts turn more easily to the future than the past and when for many the study of history seems scarcely more than a hobby or a diversion.

Yet at the very same time, there are moments in the past which seem, as it were, to be asserting themselves in the present, historical persons or incidents which seem to be coming to life in our midst, and thus to be re-affirming in an apparently unpropitious era, a sense of continuity of tradition, a sense of the dynamic presence of realities which transcend the barriers which are created by the passage of the centuries. Surely this is the case with the fourteenth-century English mystics, and in particular with the author of *The Cloud of Unknowing*, and Julian of Norwich. In the case of the last two writers the past decade has seen two parallel developments; a much wider popular diffusion of their writings – we may think of the size of the Penguin editions – and at the same time a deeper scholarly investigation of their significance than at any time before – we need only think of recent work done on Julian in England, North America and France. It would seem almost as though these were writers who had written with our twentieth century in view.

In this sense it seems important to say that the tradition

of which Julian is a part is one which is in process of coming to life in our own day as we respond to the words which she wrote. It is a tradition which is in process of re-forming itself, in part at least, on account of the vitality of her work. There is a new development of tradition going on, as more and more people discover that they are able to receive from her the things which she herself has been given to hand on. I can give a very simple example of the kind of thing that I have in mind. In the course of the sixth centenary celebrations in Norwich in 1973, Father Paul Molinari remarked to me that we were beginning to create a new kind of canonization process. The recognition of a saint was being brought about, as it always has been in the past, by popular acclaim; but on this occasion it was a popular acclaim which quite transcended the canonical boundaries between the separated Christian communities. The remark was the more interesting on account of the fact that Father Molinari is directly involved at Rome in the procedures by which the Roman Catholic Church articulates and expresses the popular recognition of the gift of holiness. At once the validity of his statement was apparent; the question suggested itself, would not all future canonizations be of this kind? Can it be imagined, for instance, that when Mother Teresa of Calcutta is dead it will be Roman Catholics alone who will bear witness to the quality of her life? Rather it will be a host of men and women of every Christian tradition who will wish to give testimony to the effect of her actions. And not only Christians; in that case, surely Hindus will be involved as well. The tradition which is in process of being formed in our time is one whose inclusiveness may often surprise us. To return to our fourteenth-century writers, in the case of *The Cloud of Unknowing* this is already clearly so. Its similarities to elements in the spiritual tradition of Buddhism have been widely noted. In the case of Julian, this kind of development is one which seems likely in the near future, as scholars from outside the world of Christendom come to respond to the power of her words, and in doing so reveal to us who stand in closer historical continuity with her, more of the many-sidedness of their meaning.

What I wish to assert is that the attempt to understand

28

Julian, in relation to the tradition of which she was a part and in relation to the tradition which stems from her, will be a necessarily dynamic and creative attempt, which cannot easily be circumscribed. The material which will be relevant to our study may well be larger and more heterogeneous than we had imagined, and we may find ourselves more directly and personally involved in it than we might have wished. We are not dealing here with ready-made, easily defined realities. We shall constantly find that our preconceived notions need to be transformed. As Ian Robinson remarks in the final chapter of his book *Chaucer and the English Tradition*, a chapter entitled significantly enough 'Chaucer the Father', 'None of this need be so. English literature is not a natural object to which a name is attached like a label; it is within our power to treat Chaucer as something other than an English poet'.[1] We could treat him as a historical specimen, instead of as a living power, a 'father', within a tradition of which we ourselves are a part. We could try and do the same with Julian, as long as we could manage to keep a suitable distance from her. But she herself makes this very difficult for us. And it seems more likely that we shall find ourselves in a much more intimate relationship with her than that of a detached observer.

I can perhaps give another example of what I have in mind; the way in which current developments are changing our perceptions of historical facts previously known, and making it possible for us to notice the existence of facts and connections which we had previously overlooked. It is a time when everywhere women are beginning to affirm in a new way their integral part in that humanity which has too often been defined in exclusively male terms. This is undoubtedly one of the major causes for the interest in Julian today. She writes as a woman. She discerns and rejoices in the motherly aspect of the care and love of God. All this can alert us to facts about her which, if known before, have scarcely been sufficiently pondered. One of the first things which must strike the reader of Julian is the astonishing maturity and assurance of her prose style. Is it to be understood as just part of that late fourteenth-century miracle, that suddenly as if from nowhere, a woman can write of such varied things with such intensity and passion, but also with such balance and equanimity? A little reflection reminds us that it is not the case with Julian that her writing, as it were, comes from nowhere. She is the inheritor of a tradition, almost three centuries old, of writing for women about the experiences and reality of a life of prayer. Unlike Chaucer or Langland, she has behind her an unbroken tradition of reading and writing in English which goes back to the very century of the Norman conquest, to that west midland circle which seems to have formed itself under the protection of Wulfstan of Worcester.

There is of course nothing new in recognizing the special role played by women religious in assuring the continuity of English prose during the twelfth and thirteenth centuries. It is a point made forcibly by R. W. Chambers half a century ago.[2] But has the significance of the fact that it was women as readers if not as writers, who had such a decisive part in the development of English prose style in this crucial period, been fully appreciated? Is this another point where we shall be led to notice the hitherto neglected role of women in the development of ways of feeling and understanding, and the expression of feeling and understanding, ways which will later have their influence through a much wider range of society? It is in no way to take away from the creativity of Julian to see in her the heir to a long tradition of prayer and meditation. And, just as Colledge and Walsh suggest that she forces us to reconsider our preconceptions of what was possible for a woman of her time, by way of erudition, so it seems to me that when we consider her against this background we are forced to reassess the importance of feminine elements in medieval thought and devotion which in the past have been too often left in the background.

But the tradition in terms of which we need to read Julian first and foremost is the great tradition of Christian theology and spirituality. I insist on the conjunction of these two terms. Julian is a theologian as well as a mystic. She is a theologian in the sense in which that term is used by the Fathers of the Church; a theologian is one whose prayer is true; one whose prayer is true is a theologian. The detailed investigations of

30

the last few years have amply confirmed the justice of Thomas Merton's intuitive recognition of her theological greatness; a woman of thought and reflection, as well as of vision and experience; a theologian to be compared in the English tradition with John Henry Newman himself. If, as Colledge and Walsh argue, she knew the works of William of St Thierry, then she was in direct touch with the one of that group of early Cistercian teachers, who most fully conveyed the tradition of east as well as west, of the Cappadocians as well as St Augustine. The Cistercians represent the last full flowering in the west of that synthesis of prayer and spirituality which had characterized the earlier Christian centuries and which has always remained the ideal of Eastern Orthodoxy. Even if Julian had only known *The Golden Letter of William*, and that text which deals with the solitary life would have been particularly important to her, she would have found there much of the spirit of St Gregory of Nyssa as well as of the Latin Fathers.

For here we have one of the many remarkable and apparently inexplicable things about her. She combines with her vision of the motherhood of God a serene and dialectical approach to the consummation of all things, and these are two of the most characteristic features of the thought of Gregory of Nyssa.[3] It is true that he thinks of the maternal aspects of God in relation to the Holy Spirit, in this following an earlier Syriac tradition, while for Julian it is Christ who is our mother. But this point is relatively secondary compared with their common stress on the motherhood of God, a theme little enough developed in the mainstream of Christian teaching. Gregory also speaks of the restoration of all things; the doctrine of *apocatastasis* to employ the Greek term. And here we have to face the fact that Julian's way of contrasting the reality of judgement as taught in the Gospels and the Church's tradition, with the more hidden promise that in the end all shall be well, is much more typical of eastern Christianity than it is of western. Both sides of the Christian world reject any kind of teaching which implies an automatic universalism. That kind of view takes seriously neither the fact of evil, nor the nature of human freedom. But the hope and prayer that all should be saved is more firmly anchored in the eastern tradition than in the west. It appears for instance in the Church's liturgy in one of the long prayers used at Vespers in the Byzantine rite on the feast of Pentecost. Such prayers for those in Hell do not feature in the west – at least in the public worship of the Latin tradition. Julian's assurance in this matter would have been less likely to arouse suspicion in the east than it has done in the west. It is a remarkable fact that, for all their differences, Julian and the author of *The Cloud* both make present in fourteenth-century England some of the deepest intuitions of the eastern Fathers, Gregory of Nyssa and the pseudo-Dionysius, both writers with strong Syriac influences in their background. To say this does not of course imply that Julian was not also immensely indebted to the Latin tradition in which she was nourished. It is simply to suggest that the co-inherence of the east and the west in this area is much closer than is commonly recognized, and that whether consciously or not she is able to represent that co-inherence with remarkable force.

Lying behind this knowledge of the Christian tradition, however she arrived at it, is Julian's unquestioned knowledge of the Bible. There can be few subjects on which those who have studied her closely in recent years are more unanimous than this, her fidelity to the teaching and spirit of the New Testament, and above all to the Pauline and Johannine writings. If, as we would maintain, her writing can be seen as standing in the centre of the Christian tradition, here is one of the basic reasons for it.

Julian then speaks out of a moment of fullness, of fullness alike of knowledge and love, a moment in which all is given. As she says, 'I saw God in a point'. This is a moment in which it is discovered that God can be known and loved, and that ultimately nothing else can be known and loved. It is a moment when knowing is discovered to imply a gathering, a re-collecting, a harvesting, to use terms of Heidegger; before and after it implies dissection. It is for Julian a moment which lasts for three days, but which then gradually spreads itself out into a lifetime, a moment whose fullness is only beginning to be realized now, as more and more people find themselves led by Julian into a discovery similar to her own. It is not surprising that Julian can make us rethink what knowing and loving are. In an age when more and more men and women are coming to doubt whether there is anything to be known or loved, she gives us new confidence in man's capacity to love and know. Her visions involve a great understanding; they are the sources of a knowledge in which she finds herself to be at one with God, at one with herself, at one with all her fellow-men. Let us look for a moment at some of the affirmations to be found within three brief chapters of her first revelation.[4]

She sees the crown of thorns and the blood flowing down over the head of Jesus:

> *And in the same showing* suddenly the Trinity fulfilled my heart most of joy, and so I understood it shall be in heaven without end to all that shall come there. For the Trinity is God, God is the Trinity. The Trinity is our maker, the Trinity is our keeper, the Trinity is our everlasting lover, the Trinity is our endless joy and bliss, by our Lord Jesus Christ, and in our Lord Jesus Christ. And this was shewed in the first sight and in all, for where Jesus appeareth the blessed Trinity *is understood*, as to my sight. (my italics)

The sight of the crown of thorns tells her that in Jesus, God and man have suffered for her. The knowledge that this is so carries bound up within itself the knowledge that in Jesus the whole Godhead is at work, 'where Jesus appeareth, the blessed Trinity is understood'. Here in a phrase is a summary of the teaching of chs. 14–16 in St John's Gospel, chapters which speak of Jesus as the one who comes from the Father and goes to the Father, the one in whom the fullness of the Spirit dwells and who is therefore the sender, the giver of the Spirit. The heart and centre of the Christian understanding of God, which has articulated itself in the doctrines of the Trinity and the incarnation, is seen and understood. And this is knowledge, but not at all an abstract or theoretical type of knowledge.

With the sight of his blessed Passion, with the Godhead

that I saw in my understanding, I knew well that it was
strength enough to me, yea, and to all creatures living that
should be saved, against all the fiends of hell, and against
all the ghostly enemies.

This is a knowledge which gives strength to pass through life
and death, and it is a knowledge in which Julian is united
with all creation which is to be saved.

And then at once she sees our lady, St Mary:

I saw her ghostly in bodily likeness, a simple maiden and
a meek, young of age, a little grown above a child, in the
stature she was when she conceived. Also God shewed me
in part the wisdom and truth of her soul, wherein I understood the reverent beholding, that she beheld her God, that
is her Maker, marvelling with great reverence that he
should be born of her that is a simple creature of his
making. And this wisdom and truth, knowing the greatness
of her Maker and the littleness of herself that is made,
made her to say meekly to Gabriel, Lo me here, God's
handmaiden.

Again Julian's vision plunges her into the heart of the Christian tradition of understanding God and his relationship to
man. God, who can make the world without man's consent,
will not remake it without the free co-operation of his creature.
Hence the crucial nature of Mary's fiat in the whole
traditional understanding of redemption. Without her consent
the marvellous exchange of divine and human cannot take
place; with it, it does.

Julian speaks of all this in words of wonderful simplicity
and wonderful accuracy. She sees the wisdom and truth of
this girl, scarcely more than a child, and the wisdom and
truth consists in her seeing that God her creator is to be born
of her his creature; knowing the greatness of her maker and
the littleness of herself, yet knowing that she is to conceive
her maker and contain him within herself. 'For in that rose
contained was/heaven and earth in a little space.'[5] And seeing
this Julian at once understands more of what is happening
within herself. For what happened in Mary in a unique and

34

unrepeatable manner, is yet to come about in every believer in whom the Son of God is to be born. 'And so in this sight I saw that he is all thing that is good, as to my understanding.'

> And in this he showed me a little thing, the quantity of an hazelnut, lying in the palm of my hand, and it was as round as a ball. I looked thereon with the eye of my understanding, and thought, What may this be? And it was answered generally thus; it is all that is made.

It is rightly one of the best-known images in the whole book. It catches us by its absolute simplicity. We can all see a hazelnut lying in the palm of the hand (incidentally, does it have its human origin in some medieval device for measuring things when cooking: 'a nut of butter'?). And this little thing is all that is made. Out of this image Julian goes on to expound with her customary balance and depth the whole traditional Christian understanding of man's relationship with God. In comparison with God all that is created seems so small as to be nothing at all, to be in imminent danger of falling into nothingness. It cannot possibly suffice the human heart and mind, once they have caught a glimpse of the divine, for the human heart and mind were made to love and know God. As an eighteenth-century hymn-writer in Wales puts it, 'The world with all its toys / can now no longer satisfy my longings / which have been captured, which have been widened / in the day of the power / of my great Jesus'.[6] Hence we have to learn how to look constantly beyond the world. Otherwise our heart and our mind will become entangled in things less than themselves, things which can never be enough for us, can never give us rest. The only resting place of the human heart and mind is in God. The teaching of St Augustine is not far away.

But this having been seen and said there is something more to say, something which Julian has been telling us already. This little thing which seems so small and insignificant that it trembles on the edge of nothingness is indeed not nothing. 'It lasts and it ever shall last, for God loveth it; and so hath all thing being by the love of God.' Here is a dialectical move which has not always been made in Christian devotion and reflection. The vision of God can be so overwhelming, the need to go beyond creation so imperative that all things created are simply despised. Julian sees the absolute necessity that man should turn first to God. 'God will be known, and him liketh that we rest us in him; for all that is beneath him sufficeth not us.' But she sees further. With great theological perception she sees God's power and wisdom at work in all things. So at the end of this passage, having stressed that we must go beyond all things to God himself, having discovered that it is the natural longing of man's soul ('kind yearning') which when touched by the Holy Ghost leads man to pray 'God of thy goodness give me thyself, for thou art enough for me, and I may ask nothing that is less, that may be full worship to thee', she concludes 'If I ask anything that is less, ever me wanteth, but only in thee I have all'. And that 'all' contains all creation, given back to her by God full of his energies of creation and redemption, 'for his goodness fulfilleth all his creatures and all his blessed works and over-passeth without end'. The transcendent goodness of God cannot be confined within his creation. It goes beyond it, but it also fills it.

We might remark that the words in which Julian speaks of the longing of the soul, 'the kind yearning of the soul by touching of the Holy Ghost', in themselves suggest how much she is indebted to the tradition of the Christian east no less than of the west, for while we may see in them the influence of St Augustine, we can also certainly see a reminiscence, whether conscious or not, of the teaching of the eastern Fathers for whom it is the *eros* of man which constitutes the essential drive of his nature, that longing for God which is natural to man, and makes of man a being open towards God, one open to the activities of the Holy Spirit.[7] We might also remark that Julian's perception that in the vision of God all the creation is included is one which could be paralleled in many places in the history of Christian spirituality. Best known perhaps is the incident in the life of St Benedict where the saint sees the whole world as gathered together in a single ray of light. But there is a description, no less interesting, of such a vision of all things in the *Catecheses* of Symeon the

New Theologian, the great Byzantine mystic of the eleventh century. The same thing is to be found in Adamnan's life of St Columba. Julian can hardly have known the two latter works, but they bear witness to the same experience.

Again for Julian none of this is a matter of theoretical or abstract conviction. It leads her at once into a reflection on prayer, in which we discover that God's goodness touches everything that is made.

> All may of thee partake:
> Nothing can be so mean,
> Which with his tincture (for thy sake)
> Will not grow bright and clean.[8]

All the means by which we can come to him are themselves expressions of this goodness, valuable when known as such, liable to become screens or barriers when taken as important in themselves. For the goodness of God himself is our highest prayer – as it is showed later, 'I am the ground of thy beseeching' – and it comes down to the lowest part of our need. Just how far it comes down, Julian at once tells us in one of the most remarkable passages in her book.

> A man goeth upright, and the food in his body is closed as in a purse full fair. And when it is time of his necessity, it is opened and closed again full honestly. And that it is he doeth this, it is showed there where he sayeth he cometh down to us in the lowest part of our need. For he hath no despite of that he made, and he hath no disdain to serve us at the simplest office that belongeth to our body in kind, for the love of the soul that he made to his own likeness. For as the body is clad in clothes, and the flesh in the skin, and the bones in the flesh, and the heart in the body, so are we, soul and body, clad and enclosed in the goodness of God. Yea, and more homely, for all they vanish and waste away; the goodness of God is ever whole, and more near to us, without any comparison.

Julian is so integrated in herself, so penetrated throughout her being by this conviction of the all-encompassing goodness of God that she can speak quite simply of the processes of

37

the digestion and evacuation of food, as ways in which God serves us. There are few spiritual writers who have spoken so directly and so naturally on this subject. We might think by way of comparison of the beautiful lines in *Cleanness*, where the writer speaks of the coming together of the husband and wife in married love as a gift of God, 'Welnyghe pure Paradys moght preove no better'.[9] It is true that the Christian tradition has often showed itself uneasy before man's bodily functions. There are nonetheless notable exceptions to that unease which need to be noticed.

I have wanted in looking at these passages to do two things. First to remark on the astonishing swiftness with which the images follow one another, and then to remark on the way in which they at once prompt profound and central theological considerations. It is said that Mozart heard an entire symphony in a single instant, and then had to sit down and write it out. It is the same here. All is given 'in a nut shell', she sees God 'in a point', and then all has to be worked out day by day in a constant round of prayer and reflection and fidelity to the original vision. A phenomenon which is observed in the arts, the giving of the whole in a flash, its subsequent appropriation in time, is here to be observed in terms of life, and indeed not of one life only but many, for Julian becomes herself a mother, and has many children. We see here something of the reason for her central and dynamic role within the tradition. The tradition is, as it were, gathered up in this instant, in this fullness of time. We see too something of the quality of the incarnation itself, 'Immensity cloistered in thy dear womb', God coming to birth in man. Julian finds within herself, finds within her cell, a large space, the space of God, and she finds all things reconciled and brought together there.

This is why she questions so radically our customary twentieth-century ideas of time and space, of historical development and continuity. She abstains from moving about, she abstains from what we should call useful and creative work, she shuts herself in. Instead of becoming narrow, frustrated, embittered, she is enlarged and fruitful and full of a sense of joy and fulfilment. She discovers in herself that the potential of humankind for suffering and joy, for love and for knowledge is infinitely greater than is usually suspected. The heart and mind can go to the lengths of God; indeed this is precisely what the human heart and mind were created for. Thus there is in her and in her book a kind of fullness which reflects the fullness of the creation when it is known as God's word and gift to us. It is a fullness which unites earth and heaven, the love of the Trinity with the most basic of our bodily functions. It is a fullness which draws into itself many strands from earlier periods of the Christian tradition and opens the way for developments which are only just beginning. It is a fullness which reconciles warring elements within the society and language of her day, as Sister Anna Maria Reynolds suggested in her study of the use of the words 'courteous' and 'homely' to describe the action of our Lord, the romance language of courtly love united with the simplest Anglo-Saxon term for the most fundamental of human realities.[10] It is a fullness which makes present in twentieth-century England no less than in the England of her own time, something of the immensity and creativity of the love of God.

Speaking of the importance of breast-feeding in the first excursus which is to be found in his life of Christ, *The Great Exemplar*, Jeremy Taylor remarks:

> Although other actions are more perfect and spiritual, yet this more natural and humane; other things being super-added to a full duty, rise higher, but this builds stronger, and is like a part of the foundation, having no lustre, but much strength; and however the others are full of ornament, yet this hath in it some degree of necessity, and possibly is with more danger and irregularity omitted, than actions which spread their leaves fairer, and looks more gloriously.[11]

Freud and Klein were not the first to observe the importance of the child's very first contacts with the mother. We can only speculate about Julian's relationship with her own mother, but it is impossible not to feel that it must have been an exceptionally satisfying one. The truth and sureness of the divine and eternal perceptions of her book are as it were

39

validated by the way in which they are rooted in the heart of human life and experience. In the promise that all shall be well, do we not hear at once the echo of a heavenly and an earthly word, the mother reassuring the frightened child, no less than the expectation of the great deed which the Holy Trinity shall do in that day? There are in Mother Julian continuities of tradition which run from the height of heaven to the depth of earth, no less than from one century in time to another. It is this which gives to her writing such a powerful sense of relevance for an age which finds it difficult to connect, in which so many of the continuities appear to be broken. If we are willing to give serious attention to what she can tell us about our human nature, we shall find much that is of vital importance for our future.

1 Ian Robinson, *Chaucer and the English Tradition* (Cambridge 1972), p. 287.
2 R. W. Chambers, *On the Continuity of English Prose from Alfred to More and His School* (Oxford 1932).
3 I am indebted to Sister Mary Paul's perceptive study *All Shall Be Well, Julian of Norwich and the Compassion of God* (Oxford 1976) at this point. Sister Mary Paul makes extensive use of Dr Martin Parmentier's thesis, 'St Gregory of Nyssa's Doctrine of the Holy Spirit'.
4 I have made here my own conservative modernization of the Colledge and Walsh critical edition. The passages are from E. Colledge and J. Walsh (eds.), *A Book of Showings to the Anchoress Julian of Norwich*, 2 vols. (Toronto 1978), chs. 4–6.
5 From the fourteenth-century carol 'There is no rose of such virtue', *Oxford Book of Medieval English Verse* (Oxford 1970), p. 408.
6 See J. Coutts (ed.), *Homage to Ann Griffiths* (Cardiff 1976).
7 The version 'Loving yearning' given by E. Colledge and J. Walsh in their translation, *Julian of Norwich: Showings* (London and New York 1978), unfortunately obscures this point.
8 See George Herbert, 'The Elixir', *Works* (Oxford 1941), p. 184.
9 A. C. Cawley and J. J. Anderson (eds.), *Pearl, Cleanness, Patience and Sir Gawain and the Green Knight* (London 1976), p. 81.
10 A. M. Reynolds (ed.), *A Shewing of God's Love* (London 1974), p. xvii.
11 A. H. Davis and F. Westley (eds.), *Jeremy Taylor, The Whole Works* (London 1835), vol. 1, p. 38.

On the Brink of Universalism

Richard Harries

Love is his meaning

At the time of the Civil Rights movement in America during the 1960s a pastor in one of the southern states went to his Bible to learn the will of his God in this matter. Having discovered what he thought this to be, he integrated his congregation overnight without scruple or hesitation. It is also said of the same pastor that when a young man known to him died, he went in tears to the mother and said, 'I'm so sad. I know your John has gone to hell'. He believed the Bible taught the reality of hell; and so did Julian.

> One point of our faith is that many creatures shall be damned – for instance the angels who fell from heaven because of their pride, and are now fiends; and man on earth that dieth out of the faith of Holy Church, that is to say, those who are heathens; and also man that hath received christening but liveth an unchristian life and so dieth out of charity – all these shall be damned to hell without end, as Holy Church teacheth me to believe.[1]

How can we believe that 'God will be all in all', as St Paul put it; how can we believe that 'All things shall be well', as Julian believed, if there are still souls languishing in hell? It was a question much on Julian's mind. 'In view of all this it seemed to me impossible that all manner of thing should be well according as our Lord shewed in this time.'[2]

The same problem may be approached another way. Given the amount of suffering in the world, was God justified in creating it in the first place? Ivan Karamazov thought not.

© Richard Harries 1985

41

It was not that he was an atheist but the suffering of even one innocent child made him want to 'return his ticket'. Presumably, however, (to speak anthropomorphically) God was justified in creating the universe if at the end, whatever travails people have had to go through, everyone is able to bless him for their existence. If at the consummation of the whole creative process everyone who has ever lived is taken up in delight then, whatever suffering they have experienced on the way, God is indeed rightly blessed.[3] But suppose there is even one soul who is not able to share in the general rejoicing? We cannot say, where God is concerned, that it would be all right if the great majority win through. In politics, when assessing the public good, we have to act in the interest of the majority against the wishes of the minority. For God, however, one lost soul is as much of a failure as a million lost souls. How can God and his saints enjoy heaven if there is even one soul languishing in hell?

What gave this question such urgency and poignancy for Julian was her absolute conviction that the purpose of love would triumph. 'All shall be well; and all manner of thing shall be well',[4] a refrain which is repeated a number of times and which, as a result of Eliot's inclusion of it in 'Little Gidding' as the climax of *Four Quartets*, has become so well known. This conviction about the triumph of love does not stand on its own. It is the spire of a church, every stone of which contributes to the solidity and harmony of the whole. There is, first, the deeply felt and long pondered conviction that God is love and nothing but love:

> And from the time that it was shewed, I desired oftentimes to know what was our Lord's meaning in it. And fifteen years after, and more, I was answered in ghostly understanding: 'What, wouldst thou know thy Lord's meaning in this thing? Know it well. Love was his meaning. Who sheweth it thee? Love. Wherefore sheweth he it thee? For Love. Hold thee therein. Thou shalt know more in the same, but thou shalt never know other therein, without end.'
>
> Thus was I learned that love is our Lord's meaning. And

42

I saw full surely in this, and in all, that before God made us, he loved us. Which love was never slaked, nor ever shall be. And in this love he hath done all his works. And in this love he hath made all things profitable to us. And in this love our life is everlasting. In our making we had beginning: but the love wherein he made us was in him from without-beginning. In which love we have our beginning. And all this shall we see in God without end.[5]

This love is gentle, courteous, sensitive and tender. There is no wrath in this love.

Nothing could be more impossible than that God should be wrath. For wrath and friendship are two contraries. He that layeth and destroyeth our wrath, and maketh us meek and mild – we must needs believe that he is ever, in the same love, meek and mild; which is contrary to wrath. For I saw full truly that where our Lord appeareth, peace is established and wrath hath no place. I saw no manner of wrath in God, neither for a short time, nor for long.[6]

This does not mean that Julian held sin lightly. As we shall see, just the opposite is true. Nor does it mean that she discounted the consequences of sin. On the contrary, the cause of all the pain in the world, according to her, is sin: 'It is true that sin is the cause of all this pain.' So although there is no wrath in God and he never rejects or destroys us out of anger, yet there is still wrath amongst us in one sense. God allows the consequences of our actions to be known and felt; we experience the pain resulting from our sin.

Nevertheless, the important point is the remarkable emphasis by Julian on the lack of anger by God towards us. He is all sweet pity. Closely connected with Julian's emphasis on the gentle, wrath-free, nature of God's love is the conviction that God will bring her safe to heaven. And this despite sin. For she knows she will sin; she knows she will fall. But she knows with no less certainty that Christ will not allow her to be totally overcome and that he will work all things for good. Moreover, what applies to her applies to all her fellow-Christians.

Though our Lord showed that *I* would sin, *I* here stands for *all*. Because of this I began to be rather fearful. And our Lord answered, 'I am keeping you very securely'. The word was said with more love and assurance and a sense of spiritual protection than I know how to tell. For just as I had been shown that I was likely to sin, so at the same time was I confronted with assurance and protection for all my fellow-Christians. What can make me love my fellow-Christians more than to see in God that he loves all who are to be saved as if they were one soul.[7]

God is unblemished love, a love which has no trace of wrath in it, a love which creates, sustains and brings us, together with all those who are to be saved, to heaven. But what about sin? Does not this hinder and even thwart the purpose of God?

Stunned in the mind
One of the most controversial statements of Julian occurs in ch. 53:

> In every soul which shall be saved there is a godly will that never assented to sin, nor ever shall. This will is so good that it may never will evil, but evermore, continually, it willeth good and worketh good in the sight of God.

This view has been criticized as heterodox and attempts have been made to trace the sources which influenced Julian. A number of medieval writers have been suggested, as has the pervasive notion of the scintilla, the divine spark in the soul which is never extinguished. On the other hand, Clifton Wolters argued that her belief that in everyone to be saved there is a godly will that never assents to sin arose from a combination of her own benign personality and the loving home in which she grew up. She had a good experience of other human beings and as she could not imagine herself consciously and deliberately doing evil, so in charity she assumes the same of everyone.

The psychology of human choice, however, suggests another explanation. First, people nearly always try to justify what they do in moral terms and before they seek to convince others they attempt to convince themselves. Goebbels, in his diaries, imagines Germans in a hundred years' time looking back to the heroic efforts he and his fellow Nazis are making. He is sustained by the image of himself as a hero. Stalin carried out the great purges, in which 28 million lost their lives, because he believed this was the only way of safeguarding the Russian revolution. In Dostoevsky's *Crime and Punishment* Raskolnikov wants to be a Napoleon figure – and to prove it to himself murders two old ladies for no other reason. These horrific examples ensure that the issue is not evaded. They make it quite clear that evil is nothing less than evil. But how is it that people come to commit such evil? They deceive themselves. It is not a matter of seeing evil in its naked horror and choosing it freely but, for a variety of motives, choosing a distorted good. Raskolnikov truly admired Napoleon: he thought the height of human achievement was to be a Napoleon figure above ordinary standards of right and wrong.

This capacity to deceive ourselves is a very terrible thing and has caused enormous suffering. But it does suggest that people are still looking for the good, however misguided they may be in their apprehension of what it is or how it is to be achieved. If this is so, then even when perpetrating the greatest enormity, there is an element in the soul that does not consent to the evil that others can recognize. The fact that even the greatest wickedness tends to try to justify itself in moral terms suggests there is an element in the soul that is alive to moral considerations.

According to Julian, sin is not so much deliberately choosing evil as the result of being fallen and blind, weak and confused. In her famous parable about the master and the servant in ch. 51, she writes:

> Then I saw the lord look at his servant with rare love and tenderness, and quietly send him to a certain place to fulfil his purpose. Not only does that servant go but he starts off at once, running with all speed, in his love to do what his

45

master wanted. And without warning he falls headlong into
a deep ditch and injures himself very badly.

The servant falls, not by deliberate choice, but without
warning and by accident. This is how Julian describes his
plight after the fall:

> First of all there was the severe bruising which resulted
> from his fall, and was hurting very much; then there was the
> sheer weight of his body; thirdly there was the consequent
> weakness following these two factors; fourthly his mind was
> shocked, and he could not see the reason for it all – so that
> he almost forgot the love that had spurred him on; and
> there was the fifth and further fact that he could not get
> up; moreover, in the sixth place – and this I found quite
> extraordinary – he was quite alone: wherever I looked, high
> and low, far and near, I could see none to help him; and
> lastly there was the hard rough surface on to which he had
> fallen.

This seems a fairly accurate description of the human plight,
burdened by the body, feeling weak and alone. Of particular
significance is the phrase 'his mind was shocked, and he could
not see the reason for it all – so that he almost forgot the love
that had spurred him on', or as the Walsh translation puts
it, 'he was blinded in his reason and stunned in his mind'.
Later on in the same story we read:

> This man's strength was injured, and he was much weak-
> ened. His senses too were confused, for he turned away
> from looking at his lord. However his will was still sound
> in God's sight, for I saw that our Lord commended and
> approved his will. But he was prevented from seeing this
> about his will, and therefore was in great sorrow and
> distress. He could not see clearly his loving lord, so gentle
> and kind towards him, nor could he see how he really stood
> in the eyes of that same loving master.

Here Julian suggests that even in this state we are seeking
the good. God knows this – 'his will was still sound in God's
sight'. We, however, neither know where our true good lies,

nor even that we are seeking it – 'he was prevented from seeing this about his will'.

Then, in ch. 52, Julian writes this:

> Kept secure by Christ we are assured, by his touch of grace, of salvation; broken by Adam's fall, and in many ways by our own sins and sorrows, we are so darkened and blinded that we can hardly find any comfort. But in our heart we abide in God, and confidently trust to his mercy and grace – and this is his working in us. And of his goodness he opens the eye of our understanding so that we can *see*; sometimes it is less, sometimes more, according to our God-given ability to receive it. Now we are uplifted by the one; now we are allowed to fall into the other. And this fluctuating is so baffling that we are hard put to know where we stand, whether we are thinking of ourselves or of our fellow believers. It certainly is a marvellous mix-up! But the one thing that matters is that we always say 'Yes' to God whenever we experience him, and really do will to be with him, with all our heart and soul and strength. It is then that we hate and despise our evil inclinations, and all else that might make us sin, physically or spiritually. Yet, when this sweetness vanishes, we fall back into our blind state, and so into all sorts of distress and trouble.

In this passage which bears all the marks of personal experience we note phrases like 'darkened and blinded', 'he opens the eye of our understanding so that we can see' and 'we fall back into our blind state'. In other words, the state of sin is primarily one of blindness, darkness and confusion. Nevertheless, all the time our aspiration toward the good is groping about, there is that within us which never assented to sin and which flounders about in the mud trying to find a way out. Furthermore, all the time, Christ is with us. However blind we are his love is about us and within us. So, in the parable of the lord and the servant Julian writes: 'Mercy and pity dwell thus with mankind until at last we come to heaven. But man in this life is blind and cannot see God, our Father, as he is.' It is not difficult to see how this understanding of sin and human nature reinforces Julian's conviction that all shall be well. We are nòt malevolent wrongdoers but blinded children. Part of us is groping towards the light, and even in our blindness Christ is with us all the time to open our eyes, reveal the Father and lead us on the way to heaven.

Christ's solidarity with mankind

In the lovely parable described in ch. 51, Julian says that the servant stands for Adam, all mankind.

> The *servant* who stood before his lord I understood to be Adam. There was shown at that time just one man and his fall; to make us understand that God sees Everyman and his fall. In the sight of God everyman is one man, and one man is everyman.

Nevertheless this servant, this man, this Adam, is one with the Eternal Son of God.

> In the *servant* is represented the second Person of the Trinity; and in the *servant* again Adam, or in other words, Everyman . . . When Adam *fell*, God's Son fell. Because of the true unity which had been decreed in heaven, God's Son could not be dissociated from Adam. By *Adam* I always understood *Everyman* . . . For all the humanity that will be saved by his blessed incarnation and passion is included in Christ's humanity . . . Jesus is everyone that will be saved, and everyone that will be saved is Jesus.

This solidarity of the Son of God with Adam extends as far as the descent into hell.

> The merciful gaze of his loving eyes ranged the whole earth, and went down with Adam into hell; his continuing pity kept Adam from eternal death. Mercy and pity dwell thus with mankind until at last we come to heaven.

> Adam fell from life to death, first into the depths of this wretched world, and then into hell. God's Son fell, with Adam, but into the depth of the Virgin's womb . . . and with a mighty arm he brought him out of hell.

> He went down to hell, and there he raised up from the

lowest depths that great mass which was his by right, united to him in high heaven.

What are we to make of this idea? Its biblical roots are to be found in the fifteenth chapter of St Paul's first letter to the Corinthians. Yet it could be argued that this way of thinking is primitive and unhelpful to the development of moral maturity. Each person is a unique centre of consciousness, called to assume responsibility for his or her own life. It is morally dangerous to undercut this by use of vague abstractions like mankind. Nevertheless it is mankind in its entirety that God is concerned with, with every single individual. It is true that he is not interested in abstract nouns but in persons; but he wants to include every person. He is the Shepherd who goes out after the one sheep that is lost even though he has ninety-nine tucked up for the night. He is the woman who scrabbles over the floor for the one coin that is lost, even though the other nine are safe.

The modern world makes us aware of the interdependence of all human beings. We are one world, the planet earth. But it is doubtful whether we have ever fully taken this interdependence into account in our theological thinking. Perhaps it is true that either we are all saved or none of us are. If we are all to be saved there will have to be (to use the phrase of Charles Williams) a co-inherence of all things. Whatever I have made of my life is not just for me but for all others; whatever they have made of their life is for me as well. 'For in the sight of God all men are one man, and one man is all men.'[8]

O happy fault

In the most impressive of all Christian services, the Easter Vigil, when believers light candles in a darkened church and celebrate their deliverance from sin and death, the Exultet is sung. It is one of the oldest pieces of Christian prose. 'This is the night' begins a number of its refrains. 'This is the night when Jesus Christ broke the chains of death and rose triumphant from the grave.' The Exultet contains the famous words *O Felix Culpa* – 'O happy fault, O necessary sin of

Adam, which gained for us such and so great a redeemer'. The same thought is expressed in a carol often sung at Christmas, 'Adam lay y bounden', which contains the verse:

Ne had the apple taken been,
The apple taken been,
Ne had never our lady
Abeen heavene queen.[9]

This theme is central to Julian. First, everything that happens, even sin, is known and allowed by God: sin is of course not directly willed by God but nothing that happens happens outside the knowledge and tolerance of God.

All our Lord does is right, and what he permits is worthwhile. These two definitions embrace both good and evil, for all that is good is done by our Lord, and all that is evil is permitted by him . . . By his permission we fall: and by his blessed love, power, and wisdom we are kept – and by his merciful grace we are raised to many, many more joys.[10]

Secondly, as that quotation makes clear, our sin does not prevent God's goodness from working and bringing from it some compensating good. 'Were I to do nothing but sin, my sin would still not prevent his goodness from working.'[11] Thirdly, not only does God work but the good he brings out of the evil does in the end more than compensate for it: 'just as every sin has its compensating penalty because God is true, so the same soul can know every sin to have its corresponding blessing because God is love'. 'The goodness of God will never allow the soul who gets there [to heaven] to have sinned without that sin being compensated. Ever known, it is blessedly made good by God's surpassing worth.' She then gives the examples of David, Mary Magdalen, Peter, Paul, Thomas and St John of Beverley, whose feast it may have been when she received her vision: 'the church on earth knows them to have been sinners yet they are not to be despised for that reason, but rather these things have in some way turned out to their honour'.[12]

Julian took such a profoundly optimistic view of sin that she knew people would be tempted to say, 'Let us sin all the

50

more then, so that these blessings will abound all the more'. This was what St Paul had to face. 'What shall we say then? Are we to continue in sin that grace may abound?' Julian puts the imaginary objection: 'But if, because of all this spiritual comfort we have been talking of, one were foolish enough to say, 'If this is true it is a good thing to sin because the reward will be greater', or to hold sin to be less sinful, then beware.'[13] Such reflections arise inevitably for people like Paul or Julian who put such stress on the grace of God and the power of Christ to bring good out of evil. It is interesting to see how Julian answers this question. First, she emphasizes the enormity of sin. It is a charge against cosmic optimists that they do not weigh the gravity of sin. In the case of Julian it is a charge that cannot be upheld.

> For if there could be set before us all the pains of hell, purgatory, earth, death and so on, on the one hand, and sin on the other, we should choose to have all that pain rather than to sin. For sin is so vile and utterly hateful that no pain can compare with it which is not sin. I was shown no harder hell than sin. The soul by its very nature can have no hell but sin.[14]

Secondly, if we truly know the reality of love bringing good out of evil, it is that same love that indicates to us the reality of sin. In other words, if we know the love of God (though it is beyond knowledge) the question can hardly arise: 'The same blessed love teaches us that we should hate sin for Love's sake alone. I am quite clear about this: the more a soul sees this in the courtesy and love of our Lord God, the more he hates to sin.'

These are the girders that hold up and give substance to the claim of Julian that all shall be well. Nothing happens that God does not permit. God is continually at work bringing good out of evil: and the final state is of such surpassing bliss that the temptation is to say 'Oh, happy fault'. Julian does not use that phrase, but she does say, 'Sin is necessary'. ('Sin is behovely.' 'Sin must needs be.') ·

51

The secret counsels of God

After Julian has been assured that all shall be well she wonders how this can be, seeing the extent of human sin and suffering. 'But while I understood all this I was still troubled and grieved, and said to our Lord (and I meant it with great fear), "Good Lord, how can everything be all right when such great hurt has come to your creatures through sin?"' In response to this question Julian is told that there are two kinds of knowledge. One part, that which is necessary for our salvation, is fully revealed. The other is known only to God.

> The other part is completely hidden from us, for it deals with all those things that do not concern our salvation. It is our Lord's own private matter, and it is the royal prerogative of God to be undisturbed in that which is his own business. It is not for his servant, obedient and reverent, to pry at all into these secrets.[15]

What are we to make of this answer for it is crucial to Julian's faith? It is not the kind of consideration with which the modern mind is very patient. We don't like to be told to mind our own business. We believe that the fate of souls, or how things can possibly come right, is our business, for it affects whether or not it is possible to believe that God is a God of love. So what can be said for Julian's answer? 'For that is our Lord's counsel. It belongeth to the royal lordship of God to hold his secret counsels in peace.' This at least can be said. We recognize that everyone has a private dimension to their life, and that this is to be respected; that if they want to reveal something of their heart and mind to us it is up to them; that it is discourteous, a failure of sensitive love, to try to bludgeon them into disclosure. If this is so in relation to human beings, how much more so is it true in relation to God. And if we feel this, how much more did Julian, who was so aware of the sensitive, courteous aspect of love. Furthermore, if, as we sometimes say, 'still waters run deep', indicating that the person has depth to their character, with more to reveal, where it is not all on the surface, how much more so is this true of God.

The wisdom and treasures of God are unplumbable. It is

part of what makes him God. He shows us what it is appropriate for us to receive and what we are ready to receive at a particular stage of our development. The knowledge we need is the knowledge to do his will. This is the knowledge that leads to salvation. So, 'It belongeth to his servants, out of obedience and reverence, not to wish to know his counsels'. Part of the proper relationship of man to his creator is a respect for the fact that not all is disclosed. In ch. 33 Julian desires to have some sight of hell – 'But for aught that I might desire I could see nothing at all of this'. She is urged to be like the saints in heaven who have no will but God's – a point which takes up earlier teaching.

> The saints in heaven refuse to know anything but what our Lord willeth to shew them. And also their charity and their desires are ruled according to the will of our Lord. And thus ought we to will – that our will be like to theirs. Then should we nothing will, nothing desire but the will of our Lord – just as they do.[16]

This trust in God's hidden counsels is reinforced when Julian enquires about a friend of hers:

> I was anxious to learn whether a certain person I loved would continue living the good life which I hoped had been begun. But this particular desire seemed to hinder me, for I received no reply whatsoever. And then my reason, just as a friend would, supplied the answer. 'Interpret it generally, and be mindful of the courtesy of the Lord in showing it at all. It is more honouring to God to see him in everything than in any particular thing.' I agreed and so I learned that it was more honouring to God to see him in all things generally than to concentrate on any one thing in particular.[17]

As it stands this is not very satisfactory and it contradicts an earlier statement. It is not satisfactory because love is particular. We are not worried whether mankind will be saved but whether John, Jane and Elizabeth will be. It is contradictory because earlier:

he wants us to know that not only does he care for great and noble things, but equally for little and small, lowly and simple things as well. This is his meaning: '*Every*thing will be all right.' We are to know that the least thing will not be forgotten.[18]

Nevertheless, although Julian's language in ch. 32 is misleading she is right to suspend judgement – or rather she is right to accept that she does not know the future in its particulars. This works in a more positive way in relation to the Jews. Julian says that though by faith she knows that unconverted Jews are eternally damned, yet in her vision of the passion, 'Even there I did not see the Jews specifically mentioned as those who did him to death'.[19]

What in effect Julian is saying is that we are to trust that God's general purpose of good will prevail but we cannot foretell the exact form it will take in relation to particular individuals.

This point is reinforced by the deliberate open-endedness of one of Julian's key phrases. She talks about 'mankind that shall be saved' and 'every soul that shall be saved'. No doubt this could be taken to imply that only a limited number of people are to be saved. Equally, the conscious ambiguity, particularly when taken with her stress on Christ's identification with mankind, holds out the possibility that the 'mankind that shall be saved' is co-extensive with mankind.[20]

Embracing hell
Every aspect of Julian's thought has the seeds of universalism in it. Her stress on the love of God, a love which contains no wrath; on the solidarity of Christ with mankind, not least in his descent with us into hell; her conviction that sin was allowed by God with a view to bringing some greater good from it; her sense that she herself would be kept safe for eternity, that God would see her through all trials and tribulations; her analysis of sin as a state of weakness and blindness rather than a deliberate malevolence, a state for which the prime remedy is the disclosure of God himself in all his love; and her belief that there is in the soul that is to be saved that

which does not consent to sin – all this underlines and makes explicit her fundamental conviction that God will so act that all shall be well. As Clifton Wolters put it: 'That strong intellect is trembling on the brink of universalism.'[21] Yet she still retains her balance for she will not be 'drawn thereby from any point of the Faith that Holy Church teacheth me to believe'.[22]

What are we to say? That Julian's whole thrust is in the right direction and that we now have the freedom to discard what she felt, because of loyalty to traditional Church teaching, she ought to hold to, namely the reality of hell? That is the obvious way forward. Julian is so convincing in her logic of divine love we are tempted not simply to tremble on the brink but to dive into the ocean of universalism. Yet there are two considerations which should make us hesitate. First, it is not simply that hell has been taught by the Church. It is that hell is a logical corollary of any robust belief in free will. If we really are, within limits, free – free to choose good or evil, God or not god; free to create our own heaven in the midst of hell or our own hell in the midst of heaven – then hell is always a logical possibility. So long as we remain free it is possible that someone, even in the very presence of the divine love, will turn in on themselves in pride or resentment or self-pity. God does not send people to hell. But he cannot stop people choosing hell if that is what they insist on doing. 'The soul by its very nature can have no hell but sin.'[23]

Secondly, modern novelists and playwrights are in no doubt about the reality of hell. Sartre gave us his picture in *Huis-clos*, a play in which four people who have no real relationship with one another and who are still engaged in the turmoils of earthly life are locked up for ever in a small room with one bare electric light bulb. In Beckett's *Waiting for Godot* the two tramps suddenly start talking about the two thieves crucified beside Christ. It matters to Vladimir that one thief was saved. 'Saved from what?' says Estragon. 'Hell', replies Vladimir. In Beckett's *Endgame* the setting seems like a nuclear shelter at the end of the world. 'Outside', says one of the characters, 'is the other hell.' Beckett's other plays also convey the idea of hell or a hellish half light in which we live. In some of them he deliberately leaves it open whether his setting is this life or just the other side of death. It is not always possible to distinguish, for 'hell is borderless', as a character in R. C. Hutchinson's *Johanna at Daybreak* puts it.

William Golding is another modern writer whose novels reflect a strong sense of good and evil. Golding has a passion for the reality and importance of human choice and also an awareness of another dimension inter-penetrating our finite lives. In a lecture given in 1980 he laid bare a part of the rock on which his life and books are built.

> I guess we are in hell . . . To be in a world which is a hell, to be of that world and neither to believe in nor guess at anything *but* that world is not merely hell but the only possible damnation; the act of a man damning himself . . . the act of human creativity, a newness starting with life at the heart of confusion and turmoil seems a simple thing; I guess it is a signature scribbled in the human soul; right beyond the transient horrors and beauties of our hell there is a Good which is ultimate and absolute.[24]

So it is that Golding describes himself as 'a universal pessimist but a cosmic optimist' – not a bad description of Julian's position.

For these reasons Christians would be unwise to solve the problem posed by hell simply by denying its possibility. Nevertheless, it is not necessary to believe that hell will always be peopled. It may be that God with his inexhaustible love and infinite patience, with all eternity to work in, will finally win everyone from their self-inflicted hells. Certainly no Christian can give up that hope, even if we are never in a position to say that everyone will finally respond. Yet this thought that love can never give up hope of breaking down the barriers of self-damnation poses a dilemma of its own.

Starets Silvan was a Russian who lived on the Holy Mountain all his life and died just before the second world war. His writings were published after his death by Father Sophrony.

I remember a conversation [writes Father Sophrony]

56

between him and a certain hermit who declared with evident satisfaction:

'God will punish all atheists. They will burn in ever-lasting fire.'

Obviously upset, the *starets* said:

'Tell me, supposing you went to paradise and there looked down and saw somebody burning in hell-fire – would you feel happy?'

'It can't be helped. It would be their own fault', said the hermit.

The *starets* answered him with a sorrowful countenance.

'Love could not bear that', he said. 'We must pray for all.'[25]

Starets Silvan also said: 'God is love, and in the saints the Holy Spirit is love. Dwelling in the Holy Spirit, the saints behold hell and embrace it, too, in their love.'[26] This we feel is what love is like. But if love is like this, still praying for those in hell, still involved with those in hell, how could heaven be heaven?

Because Julian does not go beyond the brink this is a dilemma she does not have to face. In her fifth revelation she sees the fiend and all his works completely overcome and powerless. 'When I saw this', she said, 'I laughed so heartily that it made those around me laugh too, and their laughter did me good.'[27] Later, after not learning anything more about hell than before, she wrote, 'I saw the devil reproved by God and condemned eternally. By this I gathered that all creatures who are of the devil's sort and die as such are no more mentioned before God and his holy ones, any more than the devil is himself'.[28] In other words the devil and those that are his are totally banished. They no longer have an emotional or spiritual toe-hold in heaven. Heaven can forget them and get on with being heaven. Yet can heaven forget them and still be a heaven of love?

The dilemma is this. Heaven can only be heaven if all that is not of heaven is banished out of mind. The door of the house is locked, the ugliness and tensions of the world are shut out: the family gather round the fire to enjoy one another's company.

Suppose, however, that it is one of the family that is locked out? How can the family gather round the fire and enjoy one another's company when they know that a favourite son or daughter or brother or sister is out in the wind and the rain? They worry about him; long for him to be safe. How can heaven be heaven unless everyone is in it? How can heaven be heaven whilst they are still loving and praying for someone who is outside?[29]

It seems that whether we stay with Julian or go beyond her, there are dilemmas that cannot be resolved. We cannot lessen the importance of human choice, and hence the possibility in logic and reality of self-damnation. On the other hand we cannot give up our hope grounded in the nature of God's love as he has revealed it to us in Christ, that 'All will be well' means the salvation of all. Again, if the hope persists beyond death, how can heaven be heaven till all are gathered in? For in Christ and those who are his is 'the love-longing that lasteth and ever shall, till we see that sign at doomsday'. There is this longing and thirst 'until the time that the last soul to be saved shall have come up to his bliss'.

As a loyal daughter of the Church Julian was unwilling to deny the reality of hell: yet every aspect of her thought brings her to the brink of universalism. Her stress on the gentle, wrath-free love of God, her view that sin is not so much malignancy as blindness, her knowledge that God can make our sin yield some good and her conviction that what has been possible in her own case will be possible for others, arouses our hope. And all this said, there is still the secret counsels of God in which to trust. In discussing how all things can be well Julian suggested that God will do 'some great deed'. She does not concede that this deed will eliminate the reality of hell. Yet the wording hints at unlimited possibilities, at the thought of a resolution of what now seems unreconcilable. What now seems irreconcilable, divine love and the Church's teaching on hell, will form part of a larger, graspable pattern. There is yet 'the great deed that our Lord shall do, in which he shall save his word in all things – he shall make well all that is not well'. She cannot affirm that 'all that is not well' includes hell. But she arouses in us the hope that it can.[30]

1 *RDL* ch. 32. In the main the translations used are the ones by James Walsh (London 1961) and Clifton Wolters (Harmondsworth 1966). The version by Edmund Colledge and James Walsh (London and New York 1978) has also been consulted and sometimes used.
2 *RDL* ch. 32.
3 An argument developed in Richard Harries, *Being a Christian* (London 1981), ch. 5.
4 *RDL* ch. 27.
5 *RDL* ch. 86.
6 *RDL* ch. 49.
7 *RDL* ch. 37.
8 *RDL* ch. 51.
9 *The Oxford Book of Carols* (Oxford 1961), no. 180.
10 *RDL* ch. 35.
11 *RDL* ch. 36.
12 *RDL* ch. 38.
13 *RDL* ch. 40.
14 ibid.
15 *RDL* ch. 30.
16 ibid., see also ch. 34.
17 *RDL* ch. 35.
18 *RDL* ch. 32.
19 *RDL* ch. 33.
20 I have stated Julian's arguments for reconciling God's love with the existence of hell before coming on to her profound trust in the secret counsels of God. Julian's own sequence differed. Dr Grace Jantzen suggests the following, based on a comparison of the short and long texts:
   1 Experience of the overwhelming love of God, which leads to:
   2 Her puzzle about *how* all would be well;
   3 The admonition about 'God's privy counsel';
   4 Her continued questioning nevertheless (twenty years' worth);
   5 The 'lord and servant' parable with the 'Felix Culpa' element, which gradually throws at least *some* light on her perplexities;
   6 Her understanding of the healing of human brokenness (God as Mother).
21 Introduction to his Penguin trans., p. 36.
22 *RDL* ch. 33.
23 *RDL* ch. 40.
24 William Golding, 'Belief and Creativity' in *A Moving Target* (London 1984), p. 201.

25 Quoted in G. Every, R. Harries and K. Ware (eds.), *Seasons of the Spirit* (London 1984), p. 14.
26 ibid. p. 47.
27 *RDL* ch. 13.
28 *RDL* ch. 33.
29 It is true, as Julian knew, that heaven and hell are primarily to be conceived as states of being rather than as locations. To be filled with love is to be in heaven and to be in a state of sin is to be in hell. Nevertheless, we cannot totally eliminate language about place. A mother loves deeply her drug addict son who is also a drug pedlar. But her love is a suffering love. Heaven for her involves not only her love for her son but the triumph of that love; her son's cure from addiction, the cure of those whom he has helped to addict and their reconciliation to him, who sent them on the downward spiral. Does this mean that God, who is perfect love, is not yet 'in heaven'? It means that though he is himself heaven he has descended into hell and remains with us there until 'All shall be well'.
30 *RDL* ch. 32. Robert Llewelyn in *With Pity not with Blame* (London 1982), p. 130, wonders if the passage referring to the existence of hell (ch. 32) was possibly inserted as a result of ecclesiastical pressure. The references to hell are more specific in the longer text.

He explores, in an illuminating way, the tension between God's love and the thought of hell in terms of God's foreknowledge and man's free will (pp. 131 ff).

Julian on Prayer

Ritamary Bradley SFCC

The beginnings of Julian's prayer
Julian introduces the story of her revelations with an overview of the sixteen showings together with a brief account of what had gone on in her interior life prior to 8 May 1373, the day of the revelations. Further, she makes clear that the visionary events centre on the passion of Christ illuminated by the mysteries of the Trinity and the incarnation.

Before her showings, Julian already possessed considerable spiritual maturity. Her petitionary prayers were rooted in a desire to know the passion of Christ in such a way as to enter more fully into his life through grace. She asked to have the mind – or memory – of Christ's passion, thus using a prayer which is in some way analogous to the practice of the desert Fathers, who hoped, through repeating a short prayer, to have a continuous remembrance of Jesus' sufferings. But Julian was seeking more: she wished to know, vividly and interiorly, what Christ's closest friends, especially Mary, his mother, knew when they stood near the cross. She desired no other vision. With the same disposition she wished to come near death so that she might afterwards live better. Here again, she is in harmony with the ancient tradition of spiritual guides, who taught that affliction and sickness can serve to heal those who desire to be united with God. But knowing these are unusual prayers, she wants them fulfilled only if God so wills (ch. 2).

These desires passed from her mind. But there persisted in her will the desire for another gift which she asked for unconditionally, since she knew it originated in God's grace and harmonized with the teachings of the Church. The occasion for this third petition was hearing the story of St Cecilia who, according to legend, received three wounds to the neck from the hands of her tormentors.[1] Julian interprets these wounds symbolically, already giving us a hint as to the quality of her mind and the nature of her devotion. She wants, like Cecilia, also to have three wounds – not physical ones, but wounds of contrition and of human compassion, crowned with a 'sincere longing for God' (ch. 2). This longing, as the ongoing text of the *Revelations* makes clear, was not an emotive feeling, but a stirring of the heart, a motion of the whole being towards God, an impulse of the will. Julian wishes to see God in all things, through compassion, and in a para-doxical sense, to see only God: 'I wanted his pain to be my pain: a true compassion producing a longing for God. I was not wanting a physical revelation of God, but such compassion as a soul would naturally have for the Lord Jesus, who for love became a mortal man. Therefore, I desired to suffer with him' (ch. 3).

Yet something may be missing from these first prayers, or at least one ingredient of prayer is not yet fully articulated: that is, a consciousness of the corporate Christian community in her relation to God. It is in this direction she will grow.

In a significant way the experience of being close to death precipitated that growth. For her prayer for a near fatal illness was answered, and in the midst of that illness her visions took place. In her dark room only light from the crucifix was visible, but with the showings an interior light flooded her soul. As Roland Maisonneuve says:

> the proximity of death can burst the limits of percep-tion. . . . In Julian's case it pulverizes her first universe, which was more limited spiritually; she is confronted, as a starting point, with the emptiness of the divine darkness which is light: it is this paradox which the darkness of the room and the light of the crucifix symbolize.[2]

The first revelation is a starting point in more senses than one. Julian tells us that the first vision contains all the rest in some way. This showing, which was a bodily vision of

Christ crowned with a garland of thorns, was permeated by a spiritual vision which centred on the Trinity, who enters her life in the incarnation:

> And at once I saw the red blood trickling down from under the garland, hot, fresh, and plentiful, just as it did at the time of the passion when the crown of thorns was pressed on to the blessed head of God-and-Man, who suffered for me. And I had a strong and deep conviction that it was himself and none other that showed me this vision.
>
> At the same moment the Trinity filled me full of heart-felt joy, and I knew that all eternity was like this for those who attain heaven. For the Trinity is God, and God the Trinity; the Trinity is our Maker and keeper, our eternal lover, joy and bliss – all through our Lord Jesus Christ. (ch.4)

Likewise, in the context of the first revelation Julian establishes a relationship to Christ that threads through all the showings. This is a relationship to Christ as the one divine teacher. In placing herself in this manner in God's presence, she entered into an established tradition of mystical spirituality, which extended from the New Testament through the works of St Bonaventure (d. 1274) and of St Gertrude the Great (d. 1301).[3] Of the first revelation as applied to prayer she says: 'The purpose of this revelation was to teach our soul the wisdom of cleaving to the goodness of God' (ch. 6). And she calls the showing a 'lesson of love' (ch. 6). At a later point she elaborates on the complex meaning of teacher as applied to Christ: 'He is the ground, he is the substance, he is the teaching, he is the teacher, he is the taught, and he is the reward' (ch. 34).

Moved by the impetus of the first showing Julian persevered under the tutelage of Christ, the teacher, as she grew in understanding of prayer. She did not explain her progress, however, under expressions which mystics sometimes relied on, such as Walter Hilton's comparison of spiritual change to scaling a ladder. Rather, she kept on learning in three modes: through bodily or imaginative figures, centred on the face of Christ in his passion and transfigured in his glorified state; through reason by which she reflected, raised doubts, revised tentative positions, and drew firm conclusions based on what she knew and believed, and on what she had seen; and finally through spiritual sight. Her growth was never a steady ascent. It was more like the seasonal cycles of fruit-bearing plants, which are sometimes dry and death-like, and are at other times transformed into beauty and productive life.

The first showing clearly marks a stage of her growth in prayer. The purpose of that showing was 'to teach our soul the wisdom of cleaving to the goodness of God' (ch. 6). Such an insight taught her the limitations of those customary practices of prayer whereby 'we go on making as many petitions as our souls are capable of'. 'For in his goodness is included all one can want, without exception' (ch. 6). Yet she makes clear that such a stance before God does not mean that our human needs are not placed in his care. For she says: 'He does not despise the love of his hands, nor does he disdain to serve us, however lowly our natural need may be.' Therefore, 'let us in spirit stand and gaze, eternally marvelling at the supreme, surpassing, single-minded, incalculable love that God, who is goodness, has for us. Then we can ask reverently of our lover whatever we will' (ch. 6).

That grasp of goodness moved her to go beyond the personal focus of her earlier prayers (the three petitions) to reach out spontaneously to others. She realized that she was not going to die of the mysterious sickness, since the showing was for the living, and she must communicate it to them. This forward step was embodied in the lesson of the first showing, for she says: 'All that I say of myself, this I mean to say of the person of my fellow-Christians. For I was taught in the showing of our Lord that such is his meaning' (ch. 8).

What is it that she now has to share? It is a prayer directed to the goodness of God, but springing from a sense that God is in all things. She cries out simply: 'God, of thy goodness, give me thyself; for thou are enough for me' (ch. 5). This goodness, she teaches, is closer to us than the clothing is to the body (ch. 6). It pervades all things as her vision of a nut-sized globe in the palm of her hand signified. In the nut (a word which comes from the same root as our modern terms nucleus and nuclear)[4] she sees all visible creation sustained by the maker, the keeper, the lover (ch. 5). In this vision sense does not disappear to make room for the divine, for God is present to all forms of our need, even the lowest, such as the humblest bodily functions: 'he is everything that we know to be good and helpful'. Yet the large, beautiful world looks very small in the presence of the maker: 'we have got to realize the littleness of creation and to see it for the nothing that it is before we can love and possess God who is uncreated' (ch. 5).

Julian also shares the theological underpinnings of this prayer to God's all-pervasive goodness. For in the first showing, she says, 'was included and demonstrated the Trinity, the incarnation, and the unity between God and the soul of man' (ch. 1). Looking on the face of Christ she sees the Trinity which is love; she does not see God as being (a mystery), but she sees what the divine one does in the world and in ourselves.

Julian's prayer, then, as inspired by the first showing, is not a piercing of the cloud of unknowing.[5] Rather, she beholds the Trinity in Jesus on the cross. She unveils her vision of the suffering Jesus in vivid terms, continuing to focus on the garland on Christ's head:

> Great drops of blood rolled down from the garland like pellets, seemingly from the veins; and they came down a brownish red colour, and as they spread out they became bright red, and when they reached the eyebrows they vanished . . . their abundance was like the drops of water that fall from the eaves after a heavy shower, falling so thickly that no one can possibly count them; their roundness as they spread out on his forehead was like the scales of herring. (ch. 7)

Perhaps while the *Cloud* author in his youth was at his theological studies learning the metaphor of the cloud of unknowing from the writings of Denys, Julian may have been cleaning fish somewhere in England, watching the heavy rains flooding down the eaves in a sudden rainstorm. Perhaps she had seen stray pellets (the small stones shot from crossbows) lying in the grass. For it is from such experiences that she draws her language for the bodily visions. Yet, she says, she can find no image for the beauty and vitality which emanated from the divine face. So great is this beauty that she breaks out in a prayer of joy and thanksgiving: 'I could never stop saying, "bless the Lord" ' (ch. 8).

Eighth and ninth showings
Though, as Julian says, all the showings were in some sense contained in the first revelation, nonetheless each of the other visions brought its own special insights. For Julian's growth in prayer, the eighth and ninth showings are crucial. These are the most explicit answers to her early petitions, embodying a vivid sight of the passion, followed by her own deepening experience of contrition and compassion. The eighth showing speaks of Christ's final sufferings and his cruel death; the ninth relates the comfort that flows to us from the passion, and the joy that awaits us in heaven (ch. 1).

During these showings Julian feels the pain of the passion and regrets her prayer for this terrible experience: 'wretch that I am, I at once repented, thinking that had I known what it would have been like, I should have hesitated before making such a prayer' (ch. 17). But the new insight which is burned into her consciousness at this point of the revelations is that Jesus still suffers with us in his glorified state: 'All the time that he could suffer, he did suffer for us . . . Now that he is risen and is impassible, he still suffers with us' (ch. 20). How this is true is obviously a mystery and can only be spoken of in the language of symbols.

She speaks of this insight in terms of the two crowns. She sees two garlands on the head of Christ: the first is a garland of thorns; the second is a garland of blood, which takes on the colourlessness of Christ's head. This second garland is dried out, because Christ was hanging in the air 'like some cloth hung out to dry' (ch. 17). This garland of blood which dyes the crown of thorns stands for those who are to be saved: it is the Church. This meaning of the second garland is underlined in another place, when she describes the suffering

66

Church in the same terms used to speak of the crown of blood: 'Holy Church shall be shaken as one shakes a cloth in the wind.'

In fact, Julian refers a number of times to the crown, explaining it as both the suffering which Christ bears for us and the sign of his victory: 'This was a singular source of wonder, and a beholding of delight – that we should be his crown' (ch. 22).

The symbolism of the crowns can best be understood in the light of a long spiritual tradition. Clement of Alexandria contemplated this symbol and says of it: 'For the Lord's crown prophetically pointed to us, who once were barren, but are placed around Him through the Church of which He is the Head.'[6] Clement sees the crown as a mystical symbol and explicates its meaning in Trinitarian terms.

> This crown is the flower of those who have believed in the glorified One . . . It is a symbol, too, of the Lord's successful work . . . when the Almighty Lord of the universe . . . wished His power to be manifested to Moses, a godlike vision of light . . . was shown him in the burning bush (the bush is a thorny plant . . .) On His departure from this world to the place whence He came, He repeated the beginning of His old descent, in order that the Word beheld at first in the bush, and afterwards crowned by the thorn, might show the whole to be the work of one power. He Himself being one, the Son of the Father, who is truly one, the beginning and the end of time.[7]

With this deepened grasp of the extent and effect of Christ's work in the passion Julian resolves the conflict she felt between her outward part which shrank from pain and her inward part which chose Jesus for her heaven: 'it was shown that the inward should by grace draw the outward, that by the power of Christ both might be eternally and blessedly one' (ch. 19). In other words, heaven is for the whole person – not just for separated spirits. 'We shall be blessed indeed' (ch. 21). The experience then lifted her mind to heaven (ch. 22) where she beheld all things in the humanity of Christ, and where the whole Trinity rejoices in the perfect work of

Jesus: Father, Son, and Holy Spirit, for whom she uses the words, 'joy, happiness, and eternal delight' (ch. 23).

Thus, through the lesson of the eighth and ninth showings, Julian's prayer expands to a further grasp of God's goodness. (That goodness causes the planets and all of nature to work for our benefit, ch. 18.) She also learned of the deepest part of the inner Self, which is felt secretly and which is always in peace and love, even though there be tumult in the senses, reason, imagination, and ordinary consciousness: 'All the intent of the will is set endlessly to be united with Jesus' (ch. 19). Why this is so is shown in Julian's reflections on the fourteenth revelation, especially in the parable of the lord and the servant.

The fourteenth revelation

While in the first showing the basis and nature of prayer is unfolded and in the eighth and ninth the contemplative experience is deepened, it is in the fourteenth revelation that Julian speaks of prayer at length, explicitly and fully. 'After this our Lord showed me about prayer', she says, introducing this section of her book (ch. 41). Given their connection with prayer chs. 41–63, including the treatise on the motherhood of Christ and the parable of the lord and the servant, are rightly considered to be part of the fourteenth revelation.[8] For only in these parts does the true doctrine of prayer emerge, together with its theological base.

What does she now say of prayer? She says that God is the source of our prayers for he wills that we pray in accord with what he is working out in our lives. In this sense our whole lives, and not just certain moments, are a continuous prayer and grow out of his love for us. We cannot in this life know our true Self – what we are intended to be – apart from seeing ourselves in Christ. We are united substantially to him and have been from the beginning. Hence sin, though it is not illusory, need not stand in the way of God's working out his plan. This is because there is a godly will in us – an unbroken, sinless desire for God – which is indivisibly united with God's will. This point of union touches both our sensuality and our substance – that is, the human mental structure, and all that

68

depends on the body, and the spiritual structure, that which shares in the life of God. Though sensuality and substance were broken off from one another by sin, leaving a state of disharmony, they can achieve unity again through Jesus Christ. How can we grasp this mystery? The parable of the lord and the servant throws light on these concepts.

This parable shows how in God's sight Adam, Christ, and ourselves are seen in one timeless unchanging love. Julian visualizes a lord, clothed in the sky and seated in a desert. Before the throne stands a servant in ragged clothing. The servant turns to do the bidding of the lord but instead falls into a chasm. (This signifies both that Adam fell and that Christ fell into the womb of Mary.) The lord lifts the servant out of the chasm, and he is at once transfigured, clothed in a shining garment, and summoned to the right side of the lord's throne. 'In all this', Julian explains, 'the good Lord showed his own Son and Adam as one man. Our virtue and goodness are due to Jesus Christ; our weakness and blindness to Adam; and both were shown in the one servant' (ch. 51).

Julian can now say that we are absolutely loved by God, despite our sin: 'God judges us according to our essential nature, which is for ever kept whole, safe, and sound in him' (ch. 45). 'Christ in his mercy works within us, and we graciously co-operate with him through the gift and power of the Holy Spirit. This makes us Christ's children' (ch. 54).

Elaborating on this basis for her prayer, Julian develops her metaphor of the Christ-mother.[9] The Christ-mother surpasses the best of other mothers in that he gives birth to his children not into a life which closes with death, but into a life that never ends. The Christ-mother is the mother of all the living. Consequently, though as individuals we often experience brokenness and pain, the Church will never be utterly broken. Its purpose, like that of the mother, is to surround us with the love of Jesus, who sends his spirit into our heart so that we also love one another.

Julian's direct references to Jesus' motherhood cover the range of Christian mysteries and the heart of mysticism: the deep wisdom of the Trinity is our Mother, in whom we are enfolded (ch. 54). Jesus is the true mother of our nature because he made us, and he is mother by grace because he took created nature on himself (ch. 59). We grow and develop in our Mother Christ: his mercy reforms and restores us, and through his passion, death, and resurrection he has united us to our being (ch. 57). We are ever being born of him and will never be delivered (ch. 57). Jesus feeds us with himself in the Blessed Sacrament, like the human mother who feeds her child with milk (ch. 60). Our separate parts are integrated into a perfect human being in our merciful mother, Jesus (ch. 58). Holy Church is our mother's breast (ch. 62). And throughout, God rejoices to be our mother (ch. 52).

Julian connects these insights of the fourteenth revelation with what she learned in the first: 'the deep wisdom of the Trinity is our Mother, in whom we are enfolded' (ch. 54). 'Indeed, our Saviour himself is our Mother for we are for ever being born of him, and shall never be delivered. All this . . . is referred to in the first revelation where it is said, "We are enfolded in him and he in us" ' (ch. 57). She also connects her expanded understanding of how we are united to Christ – both in substance and sensuality – with what she had seen in the eighth showing: 'These two parts were shown in the eighth revelation when my whole being was absorbed by the recollection and experience of Christ's passion and death' (ch. 55). Hence, all the insights are drawn together in prayer.

Julian then gives explicit advice about prayer.[10] She counsels confidence and trust:

> Our Lord . . . said: 'I am the foundation of your praying ['Ground of thy beseeching']. In the first place my will is that you should pray, and since it is I who make you pray, and you do so pray, how can you not have what you ask for?' (ch. 41)

God's acts of creation and redemption are the ground of that confidence (ch. 42). By prayer one can share in the work going on now:

> He means that we ought to know that the greatest deeds are already done . . . Gratefully realizing that we ought to be praying for the deed now in process, which is that he

70

should rule and guide us in this life for his glory, and bring us to bliss. (ch. 42)

One should persevere through dryness and distaste, not hesitating to ask for what is humanly needed, confident that our prayer does not perish: 'he sends it up above, and puts it in the treasury where it will never perish. There it remains continually . . . ever helping our needs' (ch. 41).

It is love which gives shape to prayer – the love, created and uncreated, which is the primary meaning of the *Revelations* as a whole. Consequently, 'Instead of telling God, "Things ought to have been this way" – which is how we often feel like praying – we are free to say, "Lord, bless you" '.[11] To this disposition of gratitude is finally added a true contemplative sight: 'when our Lord in his courtesy and grace shows himself to our soul we have what we desire. Then we care no longer about praying for any thing, for our whole strength and aim is set on beholding. This is prayer, high and ineffable, in my eyes' (ch. 43).

Hence, as a recent writer has noted, Julian learns to integrate the prayer of petition with contemplative adoration of God's goodness, thus bringing full circle the basic insight of the first revelation: 'she contrasts the prayer that is based on the consciousness of human need – and so is man-centred – with the prayer of adoration which is not indeed forgetful of human need but is first and foremost centred in God, so that human needs are taken into the offering of Christ in worship'.[12]

When she concludes her short treatise on prayer, Julian has not forgotten the lesson of the hazelnut which brought to her mind God's sustaining and loving presence in all things. Nor has she left behind the teaching that even in the painful suffering of the passion and the permitting of sin, God is at work doing all things well. All of these spiritual sights are taken up into her prayer:

I saw and knew that his marvellous and utter goodness brings our powers to their full strength. At the same time I saw that he is at work unceasingly in every conceivable thing, and that it is far greater than anything we can imagine, guess, or think. Then we can do no more than gaze in delight with a tremendous desire . . . and to delight in his goodness . . . This is achieved by the grace of the Holy Spirit, both now and until the time that, still longing and loving, we die. (ch. 43)

Through the showing, then, Julian has grown in her understanding of the basis of prayer. Nonetheless, she distinguishes what she learned through revelation, what Holy Church commonly teaches, and what will only be revealed in heaven:

Our Lord showed secrets [hidden truths] of two kinds. One is the great secret on which all other secrets depend. His will is that we recognize these to be hidden until such time as he declares them. The other consists of those secrets he is willing to reveal and make known . . . They are secrets not merely because that is his will, but because we are blind and ignorant. This he greatly pities, and accordingly himself opens them up to us, so that we may know him thereby and love and cling to him. All we need to know and understand our Lord will most graciously show us, both by this means and by the preaching and teaching of Holy Church. (ch. 34)[13]

In heaven there will be revealed that inner Self which she learned about in part in the fourteenth showing, and, of course, the face of God:

On that day we shall come to our Lord knowing our Self clearly, possessing God completely. Eternally 'hid in God' we shall see him truly and feel him fully, hear him spiritually, smell him delightfully, and taste him sweetly. We shall see God face to face, simply and fully. (ch. 43)

Julian at prayer, then, is Julian moving ever more deeply into the goodness of God and all creation, drawing closer by irregular growth cycles to union with Christ. This growth is expressed in part in her transformation through a feeling of compassion and pain for the physical thirst of Christ on the cross to knowing interiorly that God's thirst is to have all

humankind, generally, within himself. Thus she can say –
and invite all to say – 'Lord, bless you'.

Translations from the *Revelations of Divine Love* are by Clifton Wolters
(Harmondsworth 1966) with a few changes made by the writer where
greater closeness to the Middle English text is desirable for the purposes
of this paper.

1 Recounted in *RDL*, Short Text, ch. 1.
2 Roland Maisonneuve, *L'Univers Visionnaire de Julian of Norwich*, Dissertation, University of Paris Sorbonne, 1978, I, pp. 51–2 (writer's
translation).
3 See Ritamary Bradley, 'Christ the Teacher in Julian's *Showings*: the
biblical and patristic traditions' in Marion Glasscoe (ed.), *The Medieval
Mystical Tradition in England*, Papers read at Dartington Hall, July 1982
(Exeter 1982), pp. 127–42.
4 An observation made by A. T. Robinson, *The Roots of a Radical* (London
1980) (from a typescript copy).
5 For an overview of the approach to mysticism in *The Cloud of Unknowing*
(latter part of the fourteenth century), see Harvey D. Egan, 'Mystical
Cross-currents', *Communio* 7 (spring 1980).
6 'The Instructor', Book II, ch. 8 in A. Roberts and J. Donaldson (eds.),
Ante-Nicene Fathers (New York 1925), II, p. 256. Translations of the
writings of the Fathers down to AD 325.
7 ibid. p. 257. Julian's intricate symbolism, and Clement's, point to two
aspects of doctrine and the mystical life. First, God shines through
creation – for Moses in the burning bush, for Julian in the little ball.
Then, under the transforming work of the passion, God's union with
humankind shines out in the crown of thorns (reminiscent of the bush)
and in the crown of blood, which is Jesus at one with collective
humanity. Jesus' claim to kingship was mocked by the thorns; now his
triumph is signified by a crown of thorns covered with blood – the
humanity of which he is king by grace and glory. With the victory of
the passion all creation and restored humanity are his glorious crown.
8 This position is convincingly maintained by Edmund Colledge and
James Walsh in *A Book of Showings to the Anchoress Julian of Norwich*, 2
vols. (Toronto 1978), I. p. 114.
9 See Ritamary Bradley, 'Patristic Background of the Motherhood Simili-
tude in Julian of Norwich', *Christian Scholar's Review* 8 (1978),
pp. 101–13; and Jennifer P. Heimel, ' "God is Our Mother": Julian of
Norwich and the medieval image of Christian feminine divinity', Ph.D.
Dissertation, St John's University, 1980. For a study of the image of
the Christ-mother before Julian (together with some observations on
Julian's use of it) see Carolyn Walker Bynum, *Jesus as Mother: studies in*

the spirituality of the High Middle Ages (Berkeley, Los Angeles, and London 1982).

10 For further commentary on this section see Brant Pelphrey, *Julian of Norwich: a theological reappraisal*, Elizabethan and Renaissance Studies 92 (Salzburg 1982); and John H. P. Clark, 'Julian of Norwich and the Monastic Tradition' (London 1981), p. 9.

11 Pelphrey, *Julian of Norwich*, p. 150 (typescript copy).

12 Clark, 'Julian of Norwich and the Monastic Tradition', p. 10.

13 'It is necessary to speak of uncreated love paradoxically, as both hidden and known. Julian therefore describes two kinds of truths or "secrets", so to speak, in God. One of these is the being of God in himself, the indwelling Love of the Trinity which is really beyond our idea of "being" or of "love" (the apophatic Trinity). The other "secret" is the being of God towards man – the Love which is the Son of God made man, making known the Trinity to us. One is the Father, Son and Holy Spirit so living in one another that they are perfectly one; the other is the Son of God born into creation, yet so living in the Father, in the Holy Spirit, that they are perfectly one . . . It is possible . . . to know the Trinity in this life, intimately and personally (in the person of Jesus), according to God's will to make himself known. The second "secret" of the Trinity is meant to be revealed, and is revealed in Love.' Pelphrey, *Julian of Norwich*, pp. 179, 180 (typescript copy).

Guide for the Inexpert Mystic

John Swanson OJN

A curmudgeonly sometime professor at a theological school in the States once wrote to me:

> When I heard that the patroness of your order was to be Dame Julian, I resolved not to have much to do with it, since if it reflected her attitudes and approach to spirituality, it would probably be sentimental, soft-minded, and as blindly optimistic as Pollyanna. Julian is all very well for elderly spinsters, but not for clear and dynamic thinkers.

Let me compare this with part of a letter written by Thomas Merton and published in his book *Seeds of Destruction*:

> Julian [of Norwich] is without doubt one of the most wonderful of all Christian voices. She gets greater and greater in my eyes as I grow older, and whereas in the old days I used to be crazy for St John of the Cross, I would not exchange him now for Julian if you gave me the world and the Indies and all the Spanish mystics rolled up in one bundle. I think that Julian of Norwich is with Newman the greatest English theologian. She is really that. For she reasons from her experience of the substantial centre of the great Christian mystery of Redemption. She gives her experience and her deductions, clearly, separating the two. And the experience is of course nothing merely subjective. It is the objective mystery of Christ as apprehended by her, with the mind and formation of a fourteenth-century English woman. And that fourteenth-century England is to me and always has been a world of light. (p. 275)

The real difference between the above commentators is that one has apparently glanced over *Revelations of Divine Love*, and the other has lived with Julian (as we know from Merton's other writings) in an extended, deeper, more open kind of way. It is not surprising, then, that I would prefer the Merton comments, for – I hope – I have come to Mother Julian as he did. And, for me – an inexpert mystic and theologian – she is a great pastoral teacher, a theologian of essences and origins. In fact, I have coined a word to describe Mother Julian and her approach to theology: I have come to call her an 'originist' – a word which I hope will seem more relevant by the end of this paper.

Before I consider Julian's peculiar and unique contri- butions to pastoral and popular theology, let me look for a moment at what I see to be the major challenges, problems, failures and dangers which the Church now faces. I want to make this analysis first, because I want eventually to show how Mother Julian and her theological understandings speak so powerfully and so directly to the dangers we face today in the life of the Church.

There are three attitudes which have seriously impinged upon and affected the Church and its teachings during the past fifty or more years.

First, there is the triumph of existential philosophy and its implications in all aspects of Church life. The philosophical and theological manifestations of this existential approach were virtually predictable given the rationalist thrusts of the eighteenth century (and the ineptitude of the romantic back- lash of the nineteenth century), and given also the victory of science and the scientific attitudes of the twentieth century. Both of these movements – rationalism and scientism – for their own reasons rejected the significance (or even the *reality*) of a world of the spirit, a world of abstract reality and essence. Rationalism and technical science produced an effective prag- matism. They denied the validity of that which is not productive in a technological and material sense. And a third product of that revolution was the by-product of American ascendancy in technology: that is, unqualified activism. It came to be thought that the ultimate good must be productive and efficient, and that the ultimate good person was the worker and the doer and the mover. This entire movement produced a deification of anything that was sense-able, measurable, and replicable and which led to overt productivity and activity. Even within the traditional religious and moral domains, these same dynamics tend to be active (at least in our America):

(a) To 'live a good Christian life' today means above all else to 'help people'. A religious order founded to run a soup kitchen or a night shelter makes sense to modern-day Christians, a religious order founded for contemplative prayer would be criticized as *passé*, medieval, self-serving and non-Christian.

(b) The major requirement for theological speculation today is that it be 'relevant' – that is, it must be related to the current *saeculum*, must address that *saeculum* in its own language, and it must always be 'applied' theology, productive of measurable good works.

(c) Liturgy has been trivialized to the purely experiential level of the theologically bankrupt, in the name of appealing to that same illiterate and popular 'reality'.

(d) Such classic elements of Christian tradition and theology as prayer, heaven and hell, angels and devils, and miracles are either written off as amusing antiquities by the intellectual, or described with tawdry sentimentality by the fundamentalist.

Thus is the outward and visible accepted while the inward and spiritual is ridiculed and rejected. Indeed there is as much distrust of anything spiritual among practical Christian thinkers in the west as there is among the so-called 'godless Communists' of the east. We have turned away, or have been turned away, from the centralities of Christian spirituality in this paroxysm of pragmatism, practicality and the visible.

The second dangerous fact of Christian life today is that we all live with the curse of the sixteenth century on our lives: that wretched moment when in the dark of soul some reformer decided that Christianity was a private affair between the soul and God – that dire moment when the ecclesiastical versions of the cultural Renaissance lifted the individual out of the community and set him upon a tinsel throne, claiming a private royalty unchallenged for these 450 years. This invention of private religion got its economic and cultural boosts from capitalism and produced entire generations of Christians who were born, lived and died without ever grasping the doctrine of the Church as the *Corpus Mysticum*, the mystical body of Christ. This awful idea of private religion then produced impossibly romantic sentimentality in theology, in morality, and in liturgy. This Protestant repudiation of the essential corporality of Christianity is a cancer which has crept on more than one occasion into the papal palace itself.

Thirdly, we have also lived with the heritage of the Puritans: that is, a theological dualism as strong as any of the early gnostics. For the first time, Christianity experienced the separation of the physical world from the world of the spirit, with the physical world consigned to the Devil and the spiritual world the exclusive gamepark of the Elect. This fragmentation of matter from spirit was embraced by the Puritans and celebrated by the Rationalists. I recall my wise old pastor saying that the sixteenth-century reformers started Communism – simply because they placed the material world outside the realm of religion, and left it there despised until a Hegel or a Marx came along and picked it up and created the first modern materialist religion.

These three problems, then, have come to face the Church in my lifetime vividly and pervasively: the repudiation of spiritual reality by most of the culture; the introduction into religion of individualism and privatism; and the denial of the physical world by religionists.

And what of Julian?

I said earlier that I have come to refer to Mother Julian as an 'originist', because while no one has ever had a stronger sense of redemption and salvation through and by the blood of Christ in his death on the cross, Mother Julian's main theological concern, unlike that of almost all others, is *not* the redemption, but (if you will allow it) the 'demption' – that is, not the *re*-purchase of humankind in the crucifixion, but the original 'purchase' of humankind in the creation. True to her mystical tradition, Julian has come to know God, and her knowledge of him works *first of all* in her grasp of his timelessness. So, in the depths of Julian's understandings, she is able to avoid the trap into which most of us fall of putting God inside time. Since she grasps God's timelessness, she sees simple Christian truths in a very special and more truthful way than we do. We speak fairly easily, for instance, of the incarnation in which – we would say – Jesus came down from heaven, and united himself with our humanity. But for Julian, there is a precedent truth: that since God is free of the bounds of time, the union of Christ with humanity did not 'wait' (as it were) for the time of the incarnation. One of the great gifts of God the Father to his Son before all time was, in fact, *humanity*. This means, then, that part of the true nature of the Son of God is that humanity is his – and always has been his. Since God is beyond time, God's Son has (in a mystical sense) had humanity as part of his nature always. God the Son has always received the gift of humanity from his Father. And when you and I were created by God, God gave to us a participation and a sharing in the humanity which already mystically belonged to his Son. And this turns our usual understandings on end! No longer do we say – on a mystical plane – that God the Son assumed *our* humanity, but rather that at our creation we came to participate in Christ's humanity. By virtue of our creation, we experienced Julian's 'one-ing' with God. And this happened when we were created. And it was *not* a reconciliation, not a method, not a process, but a 'substantial one-ing'. And it means that the 'stuff' of humanity is already of God. At our creation we are one'd with God – and that is a fact which cannot be changed, even in the midst of sin. No matter what we do, it remains true that we *have been of him*. As Brant Pelphrey puts it in his astounding book *Love Was His Meaning*, 'When God looks at humanity, God sees Christ!'

To be human, for Julian, is to be already utterly immersed in God's creation *as part of him*. By virtue of our origin, then, there is that in us which is forever a mark, a sign, a part of God. Our union with him is not something unique which we

79

must seek as external to ourselves: not a journey on which we set out from a state of absence-of-God which leads us to a state of union-with-God. Rather, the one-ing is the work of God *in our very creation*. Our union with God is to be sought, then, not as something extraneous to us, not as a character which is to be awarded to us on the basis of some series of virtuous acts, but rather something which is true in the very centre of our being – something which we find not in some never-never land beyond the clouds, but something that we find within our very nature itself. We need do nothing, undertake nothing, venture nothing, except the final recognition of and assent to *what actually is*.

Salvation, for Julian, then, is a *fulfilment* of our divinely-created humanity, not something added to our humanity or something which requires the transcendence or the rejection of our humanity. We are created and intended and meant to be part of the Holy Trinity. We are created and intended and meant to love with the love of God, not with some weak human substitute. A soul – for Julian – is substantially and in its essence 'like God' and 'one'd' to him. Salvation, in a sense, is not a *new* experience, but a return or a reversion to an original experience – to the experience of our origin. It does not mean becoming other-than or more-than human, but it means becoming utterly, unqualifiedly, wholly and totally human, for it is in that very humanity that we find the Christ whose humanity it already is. In the search for salvation, the human being does not come barren and unequipped to ask for some kind of external gift from God; rather, by God's grace, salvation means that we are restored to the fullness of our original God-intended humanity. Salvation is found in our true created natures; salvation is a restoration, not an innovation – a return to our true and original participation in the Holy Trinity. The intervention of the grace of God allows us to be wholly and completely what our 'blueprints' called for. With our origin in the sharing of Christ's humanity, we are perfectible *because* of our very nature, not in *spite* of our nature. To be a full and complete person is to be in union with God. A human being can only be a fully human being by being within the community of

Love which is the Holy Trinity. God did not create us as
separated beings who had to seek or earn or strive for unity
with him; God created us to be part of himself. Our search
for salvation, then, is not some striving towards a future
novelty, but a *re*-turning – a turning *back* – to the unity in
which we were created. We are saved by the fulfilment of
God's desire for us. We are saved by being what he created
us to be.

And so it is that Julian calls us to look back beyond the
immediacy of the now – to *precede* the existential and the
phenomenological – and to base our understandings on the
mystical reality of our origins. 'Don't be lost only in what *is*',
Julian bids us, 'but turn to see what was intended and you
will know what will be. Ask who you are in your true nature,
not only in your behaviour, and you will know who God
means for you to be.' So it is that Julian is an 'originist', an
'essentialist' – seeking always the true nature of a thing in its
origins.

Given this consciousness of origins, and of the union with
God which lies in those origins, we must face what seems the
theological conundrum of Julian's understanding of sin. Half
the scholarly articles about Mother Julian consider this point.
It is a big hang-up – not for Julian, but for most of her
commentators. If, as Julian says, 'all happens by the will of
God', then what about sin? That's the classic question, and
we all know Julian's classic response to this problem: that sin
has no substance because it is not made by God – because
(as we have begun to understand) it is not part of the *origins*.
For Julian, sin is a Johnny-come-lately – a blank space which
appeared on the screen after creation had taken place. For
Julian it is clear that sin is a 'breaking apart' while Christ is
a 'one-ing'. To be sinful, then, is to be against one's own
nature – contrary to one's own origins. In one sense, sin is
less an offence against God than it is an offence against our
very *selves* and our created humanity. And since sin is post-
original – coming on to the scene after our creation – there
is no place provided for it in God's plan for creation. Sin is
*in*human, *un*natural and its blank space in the scheme of
things is a result of human refusal or unwillingness to be what

81

God meant us to be. But it remains an *absence*, a *no-thing*. It is not a *thing* to fear, not a *power* to overcome, not an *enemy* to battle. To see it in any of those ways is Puritan reification; it is giving a quality of existence to what does not exist; it is analogous to the mentally ill person who carries on a conversation with a person who does not exist except in the patient's own mind.

A paragraph from C. S. Lewis' preface to his *Screwtape Letters* expresses something like Julian's point of view:

> The commonest question is whether I really 'believe in the Devil'. Now if by 'the Devil' you mean a power opposite to God and, like God, self-existent from all eternity, the answer is certainly No. There is no uncreated being except God. God has no opposite. No being can attain a 'perfect badness' opposite to the perfect goodness of God; for when you have taken away every kind of good thing (intelligence, will, memory, energy, and existence itself) there would be none of him left.

That is a Julian-esque understanding: that there is nothing in human beings which is not good and of God, and that sin is merely the process of *taking away* some of those good parts, producing – as it were – a 'black hole' where goodness was meant to be. (Just as in Genesis God gives Adam the right to give names [natures] to the animals, so God gives humankind the right to accept or reject its own nature.) A sinful person, for Julian, is only an incomplete person, a person with at least some of the God-created parts missing or overlooked, a person who has repudiated, rejected or denied parts of himself which God intended him to have. A sinner, for Julian, is a pitiable cripple, an invalid, a spiritual amputee, not one who has become 'anti-God' in any positively negative way, but one who has missed out, who has left parts of the self behind, who has turned away from a portion of that God-made self who was created to share fully the humanity that is Christ's. In a mystical sense, the sinner is one who has de-perfected Christ by stealing away some parts from the Christ with whom we are 'one'd' at creation. In sin, then, we take away something of the Christ-self God intended us to be. We

82

take from the primal Christ-human a part of his nature – and so we lead him to the cross. Since we are one with him by creation, when we attempt to separate off and repudiate or reject parts of ourselves sinfully, we are separating off and repudiating and rejecting parts of him, parts of the Christ, and – since he is always bound with the whole Holy Trinity – we are rejecting parts of the nature of God himself as well. What produces the crucifixion is our refusal to accept the whole of Christ. (In a sense, he then functions with what we have left him: symbolically, he did what *we* did; symbolically he 'left' the Holy Trinity and entered into the fragmented reality of our sinful lives, gathered those fragments together in his own life and his crucifixion, and in his resurrection and ascension restored the broken humanity to its intended place within the Holy Trinity itself and re-offered us the option of our original wholeness.)

The antidote for sin, then, is the opposite of a Puritanical repudiation of the self: it is a recognition of our natural and intended place within the Holy Trinity. The antidote for sin is Christ's manifestation to us of the wholeness of our own humanity as he shows it to us in his life, death, and resurrection. The crucifixion – as it was shown so deeply to Julian – is a reminder, a calling-back, a shaking of our spiritual memories of what a human being is, of what *we* are in our oneness with him. Christ *does* total humanity on the Cross. And in that crucifixion he both shows to us our original pattern and purpose, *and* by the power of that act of sacrifice restores to us the capability, the power, the grace to be utterly human again. Christ on that cross is not some alien deliverer or foreign redeemer: Christ on that cross *is* each one of us. He is that-with-which-we-are-one. Since our humanity is his, his death is ours (if we allow it to be). Mystically, he gives us our own deaths on that cross – gives us the avenue, the means, the access to the completed humanity which was his first, and ours, too.

Just as in 1868 Johnson was able to find helium here on earth because he first discovered it in a spectrograph of the sun's rays and then knew what to look for here, so, too, we find our own humanity by first discovering true humanity in him.

And for Julian, that God-created and Christ-redeemed humanity is absolutely *whole*. There is no part of our humanity which is not of God and for God – not a single part of it. There is literally nothing to repudiate or leave behind. An example that is almost offensive in its simplicity is Julian's statement about food going into the body as into a fine purse, and 'when it is the time of his necessity' it goes out, and 'it is [God] that doeth this'. I run the risk of being in poor taste to point out this graphic evidence of the blessed acceptance of the *entire* person, mind, soul and body – even to the body's 'lowest' functions. For Julian, nothing is denied or rejected which is part of the creation. Restoration of wholeness is Julian's constant theme of salvation. And that is the theme of an 'originist'.

Before the end of this section, let me take a fleeting look at that over-examined (and usually wrongfully analysed) element in Julian's teaching of the femininity of Christ. When reading recently a play on Julian I was puzzled at first as to what made me so uneasy. Then it became clear: the Julian character in the play uses *feminine* pronouns to refer to Christ, while Mother Julian, of course, does nothing of the kind. For her, it is always, '*He* is our Mother'. But even here, Julian's position as 'originist' is significant, because (and I am indebted to Brant Pelphrey for first showing me this) if one reads Julian carefully, one discovers that she does *not* say that Christ is like our mother – but, rather differently, that *it is Christ whom our mothers are like*. In fact, it is within the Christ that we find the 'feminine' love which we then see reflected in the love of a mother for her child. It is not that Christ's love is like a mother's love; it is rather that the source and origin of mother-love is Christ. Our mothers love us with Christ's love. To be a loving mother is to be Christ. And just as we resemble him, so we resemble our mothers. Just as we are forever his children, so are we forever our mother's children. Just as he loves, teaches, rules, heals and nurses us, so do our mothers as well – in imitation of him. The maternal and feminine is not something Christ *imitates*, it is something

84

Christ *originates*. Mothers imitate Christ, Christ does not imitate mothers. The origin of motherhood is in Christ, in God and in the Holy Trinity. So it is not that our experience of Christ is like our experience of our mother, but that the experience we have of our mother is a revelation of a part of the humanity of Christ. The *origin* of good, for Julian, is always in him. Perversion or sin is always a withdrawing from him. And the pain of sin, for Julian, always results from an 'unknowing' (in the intimate Hebrew sense of the word) of God.

Thus we see how powerfully and vividly Julian's insights address themselves to those three problems and dangers which I consider beset the Church in our day.

In the face of the repudiation of the spiritual, Julian flings us back up against the spiritual, the abstract, the immeasurable. She gives it a precedence over all other reality, and calls us back to a prime orientation to those things which are not behavioural or visible or measurable or obvious on an external plane. She says, in effect, 'Don't just look at what you see, but look at what you know and at what he has shown me'.

Her recognition of the one-ing experience at creation produces a perfect antidote to the privatism of our religious culture. The utter unity of humankind, all commonly 'one'd' with their Creator at their making, and all created precisely for that very universal one-ing experience suggests the essential corporality of the entire Christian experience. Julian's constant submission of her own ideas to the teachings of the Church, and her clear declarations that her revelations were given her not for some private glory, but for the good of her 'even-Christians', are further evidences of the corporality that lies behind her thinking.

And most particularly in her understandings of the engagement of the *whole* of a person in the salvation process, she flies clearly in the face of the flesh-denying Puritan religionists. No body-hater she!

An American poet some years ago wrote a two-line poem:

85

I wish that I had died for love,
But I didn't.

So, too, I wish that I could say I had spent all my half-
century in the depths of soulful and contemplative prayer.
But I haven't! Indeed, almost the opposite, for I have been
an activitist *ne plus ultra*. As a mystic, I am almost a new-
born, absolutely and utterly 'inexpert'. So my title is very
appropriate, and I would like to end by sharing with you
briefly some of the ways in which Julian has guided *this*
inexpert mystic.

First, Julian did not set out to be a purveyor of contemplative methodology. That is perhaps the greatest gift she gave
me as a beginner. Never once did she try to tell me 'how to
do it'. Here is no step-by-step guide about what to do first
and what to do second and the like. So many (too many)
writers on contemplative prayer do just that. And when I, as
a beginner, try to submit myself to those experts, I find myself
struggling to fit my own spirituality into someone else's form.
I tried that for years in theological school and in early priest-
hood. And I constantly bothered, 'How come St Bredolinas's
fourteen-step method doesn't seem to work for me? What's
wrong with me? How have I failed? I must try harder!' And
then, trying harder, my efforts would result in even more
dismal failure. So, Mother Julian's first gift to me as a
beginner was the total absence of any instruction manual in
her *Revelations*. This allowed me to walk slowly towards her
and her work, to begin to feel around within it, to touch this
bit and that bit which spoke meaningfully to me, to let it
grow within me at its own speed, and to bear its own absolutely unique kind of flower. Julian made 'room' for me by
merely sharing, and not by directing.

Secondly, it seems clear that, regardless of the analysis of
the dozen experts, Julian is *not* a writer whom I would call
'derivative'. Her reflections and her theology are very solidly
based in her own experience, not upon an extensive survey
of the works of anyone else. I know there are those who would
take immediate issue with this, but I believe it, notwith-
standing. Julian legitimizes for the inexpert mystic the validity

of one's *own* experience of God, and preserves one from an experience such as my own in which for years I struggled and considered myself a failure because I was unable to make some of the experts 'work' for me. It was years before I found that I could speak of spirituality and the mystical experience without prefacing it with a chapter-and-verse ascription to some recognized master. Julian validates her own experience and her own Spirit-guided reflection on that experience, and thereby validates my own, too. A real liberation for the tremulous beginner.

Thirdly, Julian is a happy woman and an optimist – not the blind, unrealistic Pollyanna, but the true lover and truster of God. There is no avoidance of pain or of the consideration of suffering, but no darkness is ever presented by Julian without the concomitant and dependable light. In a world which carried every evidence and sign of absolute disaster, and in which popular writings dealt seriously with the imminence of the end of the world, Julian cast her assurance and her hope. That hope is the synthesis that cries out for the neophyte mystic against the desperate analysis and dark Gothic prophecies of our own age. There is – says Julian – a great and abiding hope.

Fourthly, Julian is theological and not ecstatic. That is, her writing could well be labelled by a paraphrase as 'ecstasy recollected in tranquillity'. And it is this recollective aspect of her work which gives Julian her stature among the mystics. There is a kind of 'sensible' quality to her work and her thinking which makes her much more approachable than some of the ecstatic/erotic Spaniards or Italians. No rolled-back eyeballs and Baroque swoons for Julian! How sensibly British of her to have had her visions *in bed*! The quietness, the containment and the clarity of her *Revelations* are far less threatening to a neophyte who considers stigmata to be a little 'far out' for now.

Fifthly, while Julian is incontrovertibly theological, her theology must be called 'pastoral theology'. It is never idle speculation. There seems to be a link to reality in her insights which produces immediately applicable learnings – even for the raw beginner. Julian's work does not hold promise only for the intuitive, or the academic, or only for the possible distant future. The first reading of the first chapter can produce fruits that are meaningful in the most simple life.

Sixthly, Julian's own pervasive love makes even the stumbling neophyte feel comforted and warmed. Julian is told in her visions not to attempt to judge others or their relation to God. And there is never a sense of judgement, criticism or disapproval in her work. Julian offers her insights as wonderful gifts – there for the taking, there for the thinking, there for the meditating, but not there to provoke judgement. One is never called upon to be other than what one is. One is not called upon to reject major portions of the self. Julian's visions showed her that one who is called to be Christ is, literally, called to be wholly and fully oneself. So I found in Julian no sense of self-abrogation or renunciation, and that was like a breath of fresh air amongst the mystics! It meant that I actually already had all the raw material I needed for the mystical union I sought.

Finally, let me make the peculiar statement that Mother Julian's *Revelations* is like tarot cards or *I Ching* or oracles. What I mean is that Mother Julian's work is written 'with space around it'. It is presented, and one reads it, and then it begins its work; so that by the time one has finished, one realizes that *Revelations* has served only as a hint, an insight, and that most of the cognition and expansion comes from one's own building upon the basics – from the projection of one's own images on the screen of Julian's work. In that sense, her work is more than it is in itself. It provides the jumping-off place for one's own thought and meditation. And while this is an advantage to me in prayer, it sometimes presents a problem when I am writing or talking about Julian's teachings, because when I have finished, I hear this nagging little voice saying, 'Was all of that Mother Julian, or was some of it John Swanson?' And I suppose that is a question which, in the end, I cannot really answer. But whether it is she or I, Paul or Apollos, it all works wonderfully for an inexpert mystic.

Contemplative and Radical: Julian meets John Ball

Kenneth Leech

In 1973 a group of people gathered in Norwich, England, to celebrate the 600th anniversary of Julian's *Revelations* and to consider her relevance to the spiritual needs of the twentieth century. At one point in the discussions, a devout evangelical psychiatrist was reflecting on the pastoral value of the contemplative character. How wonderful it would be, he suggested, if the gifts and qualities of the great contemplatives could be brought out of the enclosure and put at the service of those ministering to deeply troubled persons. Suddenly, the room shook as an Anglo-Catholic theologian, known for his somewhat rigid opinions, brought down his fist upon the table. 'No', he announced. 'Julian must stay where she is – in her cell. That is where she belongs.'

No doubt his purpose was to preserve the integrity and authentic witness of the solitary and contemplative life against the possible threats from activism and direct pastoral concerns. In a highly activistic, work-dominated culture (such as ours), in which people are defined by what they *do* rather than by who they *are*, the very existence of solitaries and hermits presents a fundamental test of our belief in the life of prayer. For judged in terms of function and efficiency, judged by the managerial professional model, the solitary is absurd. Something of the perplexity is caught in Phyllis McGinley's poem on St Simeon Stylites. The poem ends:

> And why did Simeon sit like that,
> Without a mantle,
> Without a hat.

In a holy rage
For the world to see?
It puzzled the sage.
It puzzles me.
It puzzled many
A desert father,
And I think it puzzled the
Good Lord rather.[1]

Why did Julian sit like that? One thing is clear. Her life of solitude was not a selfish, egocentric withdrawal, a flight of the alone to the alone, but a life of love, warmth and care towards her 'even-Christians'; a life of solidarity with Christ's passion which overflowed in compassion for humanity; a life nourished by a profound optimism about humanity and the world. Like St Antony the first hermit, Julian would have insisted that her life and her death was with her neighbour, and that only those committed to the common life could risk the commitment to life in solitude. No one who is enclosed within the false self, the self-absorbed self, can be a true solitary. The Christian solitary lives and has meaning only within the context of the Christian solidarity, within the living organism of the body of Christ. Julian is part of the common life: that is where she belongs.

The fourteenth century in England was a period of great social upheaval and of intense interior striving, an age of militancy and of mysticism, of upheaval in soil and soul. Externally, it was a time of distress among agricultural labourers, of exploitation of the rural peasants and of the urban poor, of sickness, disease and social violence. It was the age of the Black Death and of the Peasants' Revolt. Among the peasants and others who rose up in 1381, there was a thirst for social justice and for equality, a desire to see the end of serfdom and bondage. While many commentators blamed the rising on those heretics and 'outside agitators' loosely lumped together as 'Lollards' – a term used in a similar way to the current use of the term 'Marxists' – historians such as Rodney Hilton suggest that the social radicalism of the period drew its impetus more from the orthodox Christian tradition and from patristic writers such as St Basil, St Ambrose and St John Chrysostom, whose writings had been rediscovered with enthusiasm.[2]

At the interior level, the fourteenth century marked the climax of a process which had begun several centuries earlier, often referred to as 'the feminization of language', the rebirth of an affective sensitized piety. There was a profound quest for the inner way, combined with a fundamental optimism about the universe, features which are clearly seen in the writings of Julian as of other mystics before her. The flowering of affective spirituality in the period after the twelfth century has been described by Caroline Bynum in her *Jesus as Mother*.

> The affective piety of the high Middle Ages is based on an increasing sense of, first, humankind's creation in the image and likeness of God, and, second, the humanity of Christ as guarantee that what we are is inextricably joined with divinity. Creation and incarnation are stressed more than atonement and judgement.[3]

I will return to these two features in discussing Julian. Yet this deeply human, incarnational tradition was not the only manifestation of spiritual life, for the fourteenth century was also a time when gnosticism, millenarian cults, and a whole range of visionary, apocalyptic and what we would today call theosophical movements flourished within an age of accelerating confusion in both the inner and outer worlds.

This was the context within which Julian practised her life of solitude and contemplation. We know very little about the life of Julian apart from her revelations. However, we do know, from the writings of her contemporary Margery Kempe, that the talkative and tearful Margery visited the solitary Julian, and it is a reasonable guess that others did so too. The Christian tradition, in east and west, contains numerous examples, from the desert Fathers onwards, of solitaries who were spiritual guides to social activists and those in the thick of the world's struggles. So Jim Forest and the Berrigans gained strength and vision during their resistance to the Vietnam war from their friendship with the contemplative prophet Thomas Merton.[4] So, we might conjecture, Julian, sensitive and compassionate soul that she was, could not have remained unaffected by the social upheavals taking place in East Anglia in the later years of the fourteenth century.

Now there was in East Anglia at the same time as Julian another Christian figure of whom we know little: a priest called John Ball. John Ball was one of the leaders of the Peasants' Revolt of 1381 when the rural poor, industrial workers, and a significant number of the lower clergy revolted against the harsh taxation laws, and demanded the ending of serfdom – and, incidentally, of hierarchy within the Church and clergy. (They chopped off the head of the Archbishop of Canterbury, Simon of Sudbury, and his head can still be seen in the local church of Sudbury in Suffolk!) 'I have come not from heaven but from Essex', announced John Ball. Ball was a hedge priest, a *sacerdos vagans*, a wanderer, and it is therefore open to speculation that his journeyings in East Anglia might have led him beyond his home city of Colchester to Norwich, and to Julian's cell.

What might have happened had the contemplative of Norwich and the radical priest of Essex met? What would they have said to each other, these early representatives of contemplative solitude and liberation theology? What would have been the common ground between the mystic and the militant?

They would, first of all, have shared a belief in the closeness of God in the intimacy of prayer and of human comradeship. As Julian wrote: 'He is the ground, his is the substance, he is very essence of nature, and he is the true Father and the true Mother of natures' (ch. 62). God is closer to us, Julian explains, than we are to our own souls, for he is the ground in which our soul stands. Our human nature (she emphasizes, following the teaching of the Greek Fathers) was joined to God *in its creation* (ch. 57). God is our substance, and is in our sensuality also (ch. 56).

As the body is clad in the cloth, and the flesh in the skin, and the bones in the flesh, and the heart in the trunk, so are we, soul and body, clad in the goodness of God, and enclosed, grounded and rooted in God. (ch. 6. Paris MS)

92

In her teaching about the fundamental grounding and rooting of the soul in God by virtue of its creation, Julian, consciously or unconsciously, stands within the theological tradition of Eastern Orthodoxy.[5] Her language recalls that of St Gregory of Nazianzus who stressed the fundamental communion of the whole person with God: or, in the modern period, the writings of Paul Evdokimov who speaks of 'ontological deiformity', the God-shaped character of humankind by virtue of its creation in the image and likeness of God.[6] In *Christ in Eastern Christian Thought*, Fr John Meyendorff stresses that the openness of humanity to God, in Orthodox theology, is not a supernatural gift, but is the very core of human nature.[7] In Julian's words, that nature was joined to God *in its creation*. Humanity as created is struck in the image and likeness of God: it is essentially deiform.

It was this humanity, grounded in God, created for union with God, which Christ assumed at the incarnation. Julian would therefore have greeted John Ball as a brother, struck in the divine image, restored through the incarnation to share the divine life. In contrast to all forms of gnostic spirituality, with their mistrust of the flesh and of the common people, Julian's mysticism was earthy and fleshly, incarnational through and through. In this incarnational, materialistic spirituality, Julian stands as an early and highly significant representative of what can be seen as the dominant theological tradition within Anglicanism. This tradition sees the incarnation not simply as a historic event, an article of belief, but also as a process, a movement – in Lionel Thornton's words, the 'regulative principle' of the Christian conception of God.[8] In this tradition there is no such thing as a 'lower nature', itself a Greek and non-biblical idea. Human nature in its entirety has been raised and restored in Christ. In the words of Charles Gore, writing in 1901, Christian theology 'associates the lower and material nature with the whole process of redemption, and teaches us that not without a material and visible embodiment is the spiritual life to be realized either now or in eternity'.[9]

This incarnational, materialistic foundation of Christian mysticism needs to be emphasized strongly today when, as in the fourteenth century, many people are looking to 'spirituality' as a way out of the pain and complexity of the world. Rarely has such false spirituality been so strongly attacked than it was by Julian's contemporary, the Flemish mystic Jan van Ruysbroeck, in his warning against 'those who practise a false vacancy', and who ignore the common life and the demands of love and justice. They are, says Ruysbroeck, the most evil and most harmful people that live.[10] Spirituality and the contemplative life can never be a purely personal quest for peace and inner harmony. It is intimately involved with the anguish of the world, for it is rooted in the incarnation and the passion of Christ. Nor can it exalt the 'spiritual' above the demands of material life, for it sees (as St Teresa of Avila put it) that God is among the saucepans, a reference perhaps to the prophecy of Zechariah that there will come a time when all the household pots and pans will be labelled 'Holy to the Lord!' (Zech.14:20–1).

John Ball also stood within a long tradition, central to Christian orthodoxy, which stressed that spiritual reality must have a material embodiment, that spiritual theology and the struggle for social justice were inextricably bound up together through the incarnation. This unity of spiritual and material, of mysticism and politics, of holy and common, was the practical outworking of the early Christological debates. For human nature, orthodoxy insisted against the heretics, must be raised and restored in its entirety. And in fact Christian spirituality is utterly rooted in the historic reality of Christ's incarnation, death and resurrection. In Rowan Williams' words:

> The life of Jesus has sanctified the particular, the 'spare and strange', manifesting God in a conditioned human story. Henceforth it is clear that the locus of God's saving action, his will to be known, loved, encountered, is the world of historical decision, whether individual or corporate. It is not, and cannot be, in a 'privileged' dehistoricized ecstasy or in the mechanisms of the gnostics' spiritual science.[11]

The spiritual necessity of orthodoxy is something which needs to be stated strongly in the face of today's gnostic revival.

John Ball would have agreed with all this, and he would have added that God was intimately and disturbingly present in the poor and downtrodden, in the anger of the oppressed and the broken, in the voices of the unheard. He would have agreed with Leonardo Boff who speaks of Christ's 'sacramental density' among the poor and disadvantaged. In conversation with Julian, he might well have pointed to the terrible oppression and cruelty inflicted upon Christ. For the peasants were images of God, Christ's brothers and sisters, and inasmuch as cruelty and neglect was inflicted on them, it was done to Christ himself. That is a central theological truth which we need to recover in western society where to be poor is seen as little less than criminal. The Christian spiritual tradition includes, at its heart, the prophetic warning against those who grind the faces of the poor, who sell the righteous for a pair of sandals, and who neglect the alien, the orphan and the widow. It is an obligation laid upon the Christian community and its pastors, now as in the fourteenth century, to warn governments and communities of the grave moral and physical dangers of such policies of cruelty and neglect. In the words of the Bishop of Durham, broadcast to the British people in April 1985: 'A society which does such things deliberately and refuses to recognize that that is what it is doing is a society which is tearing itself apart and heading for turbulence and disaster.'[12] The fourteenth century was a time of turbulence and disaster. John Ball warned of woe, and, says the unsympathetic chronicler, it was whispered in the hedgerows and among the common people that John Ball spoke true.

Julian might have reassured him of the abiding and strengthening presence of God in his own troubled and restless heart, as he told her of the great suffering which the naked and wounded Christ was enduring on the roads of eastern England.

Secondly, they would have agreed that, terrible as is the reality of sin, it is not the final word about humanity. Sin,

Julian wrote, 'is in opposition to our fair nature'. It is 'unnatural'. 'It belongs to our nature to hate sin' (ch. 63). It is a violation of the divine image in all people. Nature is all good and fair, and grace was sent to save it. Again, Julian is much closer to the Eastern Orthodox tradition with its emphasis on the divine image and the glory of the human than to the Augustinian tradition with its emphasis on human fallenness. This does not mean that Julian was 'soft on sin'. But she would not allow her life or her spirituality to be dominated by the sinfulness of the world, holding rather to the power of grace to perfect and transfigure humanity and the creation itself. It is important to stress how different is her approach from that tendency in much western Christian theology which at times seems to regard original sin as the only Christian doctrine, and which misuses the doctrine as an argument against change. Christian theology is a theology not of imperfection and resignation before imperfection, but of redemption and of overpowering grace. 'You can't change human nature' is a blasphemous denial of the most fundamental Christian belief: that God *has* changed, transformed, healed, transfigured human nature, taken that nature into himself ('humanity into God'), and raised that nature to the glory of heaven. Julian recovered for all time the truth that transforming, perfecting grace, grace which perfects nature and does not destroy it, is a more fundamental reality than sin. Sin is strictly accidental, a pathological distortion of human nature, not a fundamental part of it.

No doubt John Ball would have been told, as those who struggle for a more just and more Godlike world in all ages are told, that humanity is fallen, that a perfect society is impossible, and that a belief in human imperfectibility is the basic Christian doctrine. The combination of a belief in total, even cosmic, depravity with a low view of grace is a recipe for social inaction, indeed for social autism. It cuts the ground away from Christian social action and represents a serious and dangerous perversion of Christian belief. Against the cosmic pessimism of those who exalt sin at the expense of grace, he would point to the fundamental equality of humankind, rooted in the equality and common life of the Holy

96

Trinity. He saw the Holy Trinity as the basis of the new world order. As in the Holy Trinity, so on earth: none is afore or after other, none is greater or less than another. If human beings shared the divine image, then they shared the common life and the inner equality of the divine being.

So, on the 13 July 1381, the feast of Corpus Christi, John Ball preached his memorable sermon on Blackheath in south London, in which he warned: 'Things cannot go well in England, nor ever shall, till all be held common; till there be not bond and free but we all are of one condition.' He rooted that belief in human equality in his understanding of the nature of God, and, significantly, in the account of Adam and Eve, created in the image of God. Were we not all children of these original parents, he asked. Inequality in wealth and status did not exist in Paradise, for

> When Adam delved and Eve span,
> Who was then the gentleman?

We find John Ball's words and themes picked up later by the radical movements of the English Civil War period, the Levellers, the Diggers and the Fifth Monarchy Men. In language which recalls John Ball's sermon, Gerrard Winstanley speaks of the created order as the 'clothing of God', of the earth as a 'common storehouse', and of Christ's presence among the poor, for 'he takes up his abode in a manger in and amongst the poor in spirit and the despised ones of the earth'.[13]

Julian of Norwich and John Ball shared a high view of human nature and of human potential, a view of humanity as sharing God's image, rooted and enfolded in the divine ground. Humanity is 'fundamentally rooted in God's eternal love'. Like John Ball, Julian saw the divine purpose expressed in the most basic physical functions: in one manuscript she speaks of the process of excretion as the work of God who does not 'disdain to serve us in the simplest natural functions of the body'.[14] Similarly, John Ball rejected the sharp dualism of spirit and matter which sought to protect God from flesh and from the struggles of humanity. Both Julian and John lived at a time when, as in our day, gnostic and occult spiritual movements were undergoing a renaissance. They were thoroughgoing incarnationalists and Christian materialists, believing that what has not been assumed has not been healed. At the heart of their spirituality was the Eucharist, the sacramental manifestation of the common life, the *koinōnia*. The Christian Eucharist stands as a permanent protest against private, de-materialized, elitist spirituality, for it roots its mystical vision in the social, physical, common, shared reality of eating and drinking. John Ball and his followers drew radical consequences from the eucharistic sharing: they saw it as a pointer towards a more eucharistic world in which resources were truly offered, consecrated, divided and shared. The Eucharist for them was a living symbol of how human society could be refashioned. They would have agreed with the nineteenth-century Anglican writer Stewart Headlam that those who assist at holy communion are bound to be holy communists.[15]

Finally, Julian and John Ball would have shared that divinely inspired optimism expressed in Julian's memorable words: 'All shall be well, and all shall be well, and all manner of thing shall be well.' Julian might have strengthened John Ball with such words as these. For the future to him must have seemed bleak. He was soon to meet his death, with the peasant rising crushed. Things would not go well in England. Many less optimistic souls would have given up the struggle as hopeless. Neither Julian nor John Ball were fatalists: neither was naive about the easy perfectibility of human beings or human society. Yet both held firmly to an unshakeable conviction that God was in control, that human beings and human society were not doomed, that God was mending his broken creation. This belief that God is at work within human history, within the upheavals and crises of nations and peoples, is the heart of the prophetic tradition. The New Testament symbol for the belief is the Kingdom of God. To discern the ways in which God is bringing in the Kingdom, to discern the signs of the times, to recognize, and cooperate with, the working out of God's purpose within history, is a central task of Christian spirituality. This is why contemplation and prophecy must always go together, for without the contemplative vision, the sun goes down on the prophets. Prophecy and action are born from, and constantly nourished and sustained by, vision. But vision must be vision of reality, involving a deepened awareness of the anguish of the world, and of what is happening to the images of God. Julian of Norwich and John Ball need each other badly. Contemplatives and activists need to hold close to each other, to nourish, to interrogate, to disturb, confront, and sustain each other.

Of course, there is not a shred of evidence that this meeting ever took place. But we do know that over the centuries contemplatives and activists, mystics and militants, seekers after personal and political liberation, have talked with, and gained nourishment and insight from, each other. We know too that Christian spirituality, at its best seeks to unite interior and exterior struggles and cares, rooted as it is in the materiality of incarnation, resurrection and Eucharist. We know too that in our own day, among Christians of many traditions, the false polarizing of spirituality and social justice is being overcome, and that the ending of the related false polarity of personal and political remains one of our most urgent theological and pastoral tasks at the end of the twentieth century. Central to this task is the recovery of Christological orthodoxy and of the good news of the Kingdom of God.

For we know also the subtle temptations for spirituality and politics to be driven apart by those who seek a private ecstasy and those who wish to maintain power, untroubled by religious interference. We know that, in our day, 'spirituality' is being marketed as a diversion, a form of inner excitement, a devotional commodity which in no way disturbs, upsets or affects the established order. We know that spirituality can easily become a way of escape from the living God who continues to confront and trouble us in the desperate and anguished faces of the broken and dehumanized people of the back streets. We need to learn from Julian that spirituality must be human, natural, earthy, and joyful: and from John Ball that it must be related to, and tested against, the experiences and sufferings of the common people.

In our own discipleship the encounter must take place

99

between the recognition of the presence of God in the depths of the soul, and the recognition of his presence in the poor and downtrodden; between the awareness of the terrible reality of personal and structural sin, and the awareness of the potential Godlikeness, the 'ontological deiformity', of the human person and the human community; between the recognition of the destructive forces in the world, and of the reality of the Kingdom of God as a sure and certain hope; between the vision of God and the anguish of the world.

If these encounters take place in us, Julian of Norwich and John Ball, the contemplative and the radical prophet, will truly have met.

1 Phyllis McGinley, *Times Three* (New York 1975), pp. 46–7.
2 See Rodney Hilton, *Bond Men Made Free: medieval peasant movements and the English Rising of 1381* (London 1977 edn.). Hilton claims that 'the better they knew the Bible and the writings of the Fathers of the Church the more explosive the mixture of social and religious radicalism was likely to be' (p. 210). Of John Ball, he notes that 'his reported sayings are in the long tradition of Christian social radicalism which goes back to St Ambrose of Milan if not before' (p. 211).
3 Caroline Walker Bynum, *Jesus as Mother: studies in the spirituality of the High Middle Ages* (Berkeley, Los Angeles, and London 1982), p. 130.
4 For some reflections on Merton by his friends, see Paul Wilkes (ed.), *Merton by those who knew him* (San Francisco 1984).
5 Brant Pelphrey, *Love Was His Meaning: the theology and mysticism of Julian of Norwich* (Salzburg 1982). Pelphrey says that Julian's work 'draws together the important strands of Christian spirituality as it is found in both the western Catholic mystics and in Eastern Orthodoxy' (p. x.).
6 Paul Evdokimov, *L'Orthodoxie* (Neuchatel 1959), p. 88.
7 John Meyendorff, *Christ in Eastern Christian Thought* (New York 1975), p. 11.
8 L. S. Thornton, *The Incarnate Lord* (London 1928), p. 7.
9 Charles Gore, *The Body of Christ* (London 1901), p. 39.
10 Jan van Ruysbroeck, *The Book of Supreme Truth*, ch. 4. See also *The Adornment of the Spiritual Marriage*, ch. 66.
11 Rowan Williams, *The Wound of Knowledge* (London 1979), p..30.
12 David Jenkins, 'The God of freedom and the freedom of God', The Hibbert Lecture 1985, *The Listener* (18 April 1985), pp. 14–17.
13 G. H. Sabine (ed.) *The Works of Gerrard Winstanley* (New York 1941), pp. 190, 251–2, 473–4. See also Christopher Hill, *The World Turned Upside Down: radical ideas during the English Revolution* (London 1972).

14 *RDL* ch. 6 (Paris MS). Here and elsewhere I have used the translation of E. Colledge and J. Walsh (London and New York 1978).
15 Stewart Headlam, *The Laws of Eternal Life* (London 1888), p. 52.

God alone Suffices

Elizabeth Ruth Obbard ODC

When I first read the *Revelations* of Julian my immediate reaction was not so much 'what a deep understanding of God is in these pages' as 'what an amazing person!' For despite the amount Julian has to say of her showings, and the comparatively little she tells us of herself, we have the inescapable impression that the writer is a very real human being with a pronounced womanly intuition and eye for detail. And the next thing that flashed into my mind was 'how very similar Julian is to Teresa of Avila, that down-to-earth, matter-of-fact saint of sixteenth-century Spain of whom we know so much'. Outwardly of course it may seem that they are totally separated by language, culture, tradition, but in fact there is much that links them beside their practical interpretation of extraordinary prayer-experiences.

We tend to think of Teresa as the charismatic foundress, the Madre of the Carmelites, but her background is far removed from the monastic environment in which our imagination too easily ensconces her. Both Julian and Teresa were the product of a milieu of independent religious women, whose piety was formed by deep personal devotion to the Saviour, rather than by the liturgical peace and stability of medieval monasticism. Julian, as an anchoress, had previously lived as a devout woman in the world; hers is a very individual approach to Christ. But Teresa, who entered the Carmel of the Incarnation at the age of twenty-one, found herself in similar company, even though at low spiritual ebb, for her convent had begun as a beatorio, or béguinage, and was not rooted in the Benedictine tradition of a settled, regular life such as might be found in the great abbeys and priories of the period; it had evolved merely from a small group of single women who wished to live a life of devotion. Although the Rule of St Albert was adopted as a basic guide (and to keep the community from ecclesiastical suspicion) it was hardly adhered to with rigour. Each nun had a great deal of freedom, her own room, her own little kitchen, could entertain friends in her quarters and go in and out at will. The former béguinage was an observant convent in name only. It could be more appropriately designated a group of 'pious ladies'.

When at about the age of thirty-eight Teresa came to her senses and decided that this leisurely life was not the soil in which saints are nurtured she resolved to infuse new vigour into the Rule she was already vowed to follow, and which favoured an eremitical spirit, its central clause being 'Each of you is to stay in his own cell or nearby, pondering the Lord's law day and night and keeping watch at his prayers'. For this purpose she founded the first of many subsequent Carmels where strict enclosure and solitary prayer were combined with a warm, supportive community life. In striving to set up a climate for continual prayer she was, in some way, placing each sister in an interior anchorhold, for Teresa held up the ancient hermits of Mount Carmel as her primary inspiration:

> We . . . are called to prayer and contemplation. This was the object of our Order, to this lineage we belong. Our holy Fathers . . . sought in perfect solitude and utter contempt of the world for this treasure, this priceless pearl of which we speak, and we are their descendants. (*Interior Castle* Mansion 5)

She inculcated a very personal prayer life. Jesus was to be the supreme Friend of her sisters. They were to live always with and for him. She envisaged their following Christ in solitude, and she therefore legislated for a strict reclusion and controlled environment where all energies could be directed towards the Lord.

Teresa herself was a very natural and maternal woman;

103

she wanted her nuns to be cheeful and spontaneous, the
numbers small, the surroundings simple, the work diligently
attended to. To facilitate intimacy with God was her aim,
allowing each nun to pursue the attractions of grace. While
living in community each was 'Alone with the Alone'. Her
famous 'God alone suffices' is an echo of Julian's 'You are
enough for me'. This is the basis of both women's spirituality,
rooted as it is in the hermit tradition and the response to God
in solitude.

Julian and Teresa are both what modern psychologists
would term 'sensitives'. They have about them a note of joy
and optimism, a strong sense of affinity with the human and
transcendent aspects of themselves and others, and this is
clothed for them in visions – they 'see'. However, like all
genuine mystics, they stress, with John of the Cross, that
seeing is not essential, *being* is. Julian relates explicitly that one
is blessed for living by faith and love, not by sight;[1] and
Teresa continually returns to a theme which runs through all
her writings – that the *only* proof of prayer's reality is its effect
on our lives. Even in the seventh mansion, which she terms
the goal of union, she insists: 'This, my sisters, is what I
would have us strive for . . . not for our own enjoyment but
to gain strength to serve God . . . This is the reason of the
spiritual marriage whose children are always good works.'
Both women are emphatic that while they hope to enlighten
others with what they have to say, and that they must 'say
as they see', this is not the kernel of faith, nor have they any
real advantage over the common Christian, for *all* have the
Church, the sacraments, the Lord's Gospel, and these are
fully sufficient. They have been given what a modern writer,
Ruth Burrows, would term 'light-on' experiences: Julian, one
light-on experience with deep psychic effects, a source of
inspiration and meditation for the remainder of her life;
Teresa, more constant experiences with a variety of psychic
echoes. Now, these are *not* necessarily mystical graces of a
superior order to those which others can have. The reality of
grace can be present, and usually is, without any
accompanying phenomena, but by some mysterious inner
faculty these women have been made aware of God's

'holding', and want to communicate this knowledge to others; they have 'felt' his touch, 'seen' him present. However, this, as they well know, is a gift given *for* others *through* them, that Christians may believe and be strengthened. The 'holding' is equally real for those who feel, experience nothing on the conscious level; they are enveloped in dark faith but God's supporting hand is no less secure. The revelations granted to seers are no 'proof' of anything (they might be the result of an over-active imagination or some psychological flaw) unless the one so favoured lives more from the centre of love and refuses all self-glorification. That is why Julian and Teresa are so refreshing in their simplicity; we are conscious of being in contact with robust minds, far more concerned with God and his mystery than with themselves. They have the good sense to know that he can make use of them as a potter uses his clay (Jer. 18:6). They realize they have nothing to glory in except God's mercy.

Hence, both are women who use their minds on what they see – what has been granted passively is actively made their own; there is power and thrust in their courageous pondering that makes us gasp with delight, and resolve to try and think through some of the trains of thought they set us on. But they are never *merely* speculative; they are always drawing practical applications for ordinary life, never permitting us to be involved on an intellectual level alone, challenging us to get down to do what we can to respond to God's invitation to take over our own lives. They *see* God is enough, and their aim is to help us *believe* this and act on it, then we shall *know* for ourselves.

Julian is more of a theologian in my opinion because she concerns herself with ultimate questions in an original way – incarnation, redemption, sin, judgement; Teresa is more of a spiritual directress. This difference is due not only to historical circumstances (Teresa lived and wrote during the Counter-Reformation in Spain with the shadow of the Inquisition behind her), but rather to differences in temperament. While both are women of deep prayer and psychic gifts they have very personal ways of interpreting their visions according to their temperamental make-up. Teresa is socially minded,

105

interested in the relevance of her experiences to others who follow the paths of solitary prayer; Julian is more concerned with the nature of God himself (although she draws many practical conclusions from her thinking). Teresa wants to guide and direct, Julian to comfort and sustain.

There is of course neither time nor space to correlate all the similar and diverse aspects of their teaching; but perhaps I could begin by pointing out that both are involved not with a certain type of 'religious perfection' suitable only for people who have taken upon themselves a monastic way of life (for, as I have said, neither came from this kind of background) but rather they are desirous of sharing with others what they see as basic to *all* serious Christian living. The man, Jesus, is their focal point, and companionship with him is nourished by prayer and active compassion for one's neighbour. While we must 'work away at our praying', the active social corollary is also an inescapable ingredient, for how can we look at Christ and not long to be like him? That means living as he did, open to the Father and to others, spurning all selfish concerns. Active compassion, especially in Teresa, is linked with strength, and has nothing to do with sweetness and softness as many seem to imagine.

I would like to concentrate on Julian's first revelation, for, as she says, it is the basic revelation upon which, as it were, the others are but an expanded commentary. I see that the conclusions she draws from this 'showing' are entirely in accord with the three practical points Teresa enunciates in the *Way of Perfection* as a foundation for prayer, and which she accounts vital for all Christian life – for in Teresa's eyes Christian life without prayer can exist only as an abstract notion! These three things, Teresa says, are 'One . . . love for each other; the second, detachment from all created things; the third, true humility, which, although I put it last, is the most important of the three and embraces all the rest'.[2] Without these a 'spiritual life' is pure sham.

Let us note first that Julian and Teresa find the path to relationship with and knowledge of God through the humanity of Jesus. In other words, the first step of the soul is to contemplate Christ, and this they do by means of a 'picture', described in more or less detail. Julian gives us her very vivid glimpse of the bleeding head; Teresa describes things more tersely:

> One day, when I was at prayer, the Lord was pleased to reveal to me nothing but his hands, the beauty of which was so great as to be indescribable. This made me very fearful, as does every new experience that I have when the Lord is beginning to grant me some supernatural favour. A few days later I also saw that divine face, which seemed to leave me completely absorbed.[3]

From the contemplation of Christ they are then led to an insight into the nature of God and his dealings with men. This of course has a firm scriptural foundation. Jesus himself has said, 'no one comes to the Father but by me. He who sees me has seen the Father'. From God, Julian and Teresa then move into how the vision teaches us about his relationship towards us, and lastly some practical conclusions are drawn. This is the 'way in' to the divinty for all. All who are serious Christians are called to be mystics in the deepest sense of the word, their soul cleaving to God in union of wills, and in classical mystical works the first step is invariably meditation upon Christ – through active imagination, Gospel reading, study. From Christ we receive an insight into the Father, and then through the Spirit we are enabled to conform our lives to like living and loving. Whether the 'seeing' takes place in the darkness of faith or the clarity of 'vision' matters not at all. The mystical life, envisaged as a life of union with God, is a life of love, and of this the only proof is conformity of our will with that of God. So-called 'mystical experiences' are no guarantee of God's predilection; in fact Julian and Teresa both point this out unequivocally:

> Because of this showing, I am not good; I am only good if I love God better. If you love God better than I do, you are that much better than I am . . . for I am sure there are many who never had sign or showing, except for the ordinary teaching of Holy Church, who love God better than I do. (Julian)[4]

If you want to know whether you have made progress or not, you may be sure that you have if each of you . . . [acts] for the profit and benefit of the rest. Progress has nothing to do with enjoying the greatest number of consolations in prayer, or with raptures, visions or favours often given by the Lord, the value of which we cannot estimate until we reach the world to come. The other things I have been describing are current coin . . . not . . . like those favours which are given us and then come to an end. (Teresa)[5]

Neither 'favours' nor adherence to law and an upright moral life are the equivalent of actually living in intimacy with God. This is effected only by love, enshrined in the *effective* desire to do absolutely everything in accord with his will. Like Jesus, the Father's will must be the only object of our longing, our only nourishment. We need not envy Julian or Teresa or others like them their 'experiences'. The deepest reality, as they themselves are convinced, is open to us all. What we learn from them can give us comfort and encouragement, but ultimately we have each personally to take God at his word, and make him our only centre.

The first revelation

Julian introduces the first revelation by saying that it 'tells of Christ's precious crowning with thorns. It included and demonstrated the Trinity, the incarnation, and the unity between God and the soul of man. There were many splendid revelations of eternal wisdom and many lovely lessons about love, and all the subsequent revelations are based on these'. Surely a most inclusive description that could scarcely be surpassed! In this we get a glimpse of Julian's powerful mind at work to synthesize and correllate all that she knows and understands after years of solitary reflection. The flower has blossomed from the tiny seed, just as in each experience of ours there is present, albeit concealed, the whole of our history and future destiny. To contemplate is to pierce the shell of experience and feed on its kernel, God's wisdom and providence.

The shell of the first revelation is the crucifix Julian beholds when she lies, sick unto death, in her room. As she penetrates deeper into the meaning of the living death of the Son of God so she pierces to the kernel, the ineffable mystery of the Trinity, and all that this means for our humanity. Then she returns to the outer world once more, drawing conclusions about all she has understood. There is a circular movement expressed thus:

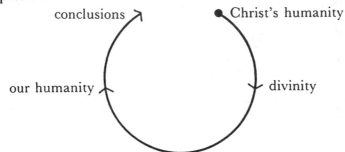

What Julian learns about the divinity and our relations with it are buried in the heart, below the surface of life; Christ's humanity is the way in, and the result of 'entering into Christ' leads to definite guidelines which affect the exterior way we live. St Teresa and in fact all Christian mystics delineate a similar route.

Contemplation of the man Jesus
The passion has always been considered the pre-eminent way in which to discover the Lord, for it portrays him at the consummating moment of love – fully realized and made visible for us in his painful death. Julian's vision of the crowned and suffering Saviour evokes not so much *our* horror as *his* Majesty. She describes the vision graphically in ch. 4, and her 'seeing' is concentrated upon the head. (Interestingly, this concentration on one aspect of the physical Christ Teresa ascribes to our inability to take in the whole body except by degrees,[6] and St Gertrude, in her well-known 'Salutation of all the Sacred Limbs of Jesus', follows exactly the same pattern, working up gradually to the exclamation 'Hail, whole Body of my Jesus, hanged for us upon the cross, torn and wounded, dead and buried'.) Contemplating the whole Christ by means

of one symbol is not only medieval; it has been revived in more recent times, first by devotion to the Sacred Heart, and secondly in that aspect so dear to Thérèse of Lisieux – the Holy Face. Thérèse in fact discovered a basis for her whole spirituality in this face, 'without beauty, without majesty', and made it the pivotal point of her own interpretation of life. She writes in her poems:

Your Face is now my sole possession
I shall ask nothing but this treasure,
hiding myself in you from all fame.
I will be like you my Jesus . . .
Imprint on me the divine image, the gentle features
so that I may be holy.
Soon their imprints will make me
so I will draw all hearts to you.

For Julian, the 'precious crowning', through which she was enabled to enter into the meaning of the whole passion, carries with it reminiscences of kingship. Christ crowned is 'his Majesty' as Teresa loved to call him. In the words of the traditional hymn Vexilla Regis, 'Tell the nations, Christ *reigns* from the tree'. The crown of thorns is a 'garland' for him who, in his crucifixion, takes the church as his bride, betrothed in blood and water. In Scripture, 'garland' is associated with both kingship (S. of S. 3:11) and marriage (Isa. 61:10); transformed in glory it is the laurel wreath of the conqueror (Heb. 2:9). As I see it, in Julian's 'garland' there is an unconscious intertwining of what pervades her entire teaching – the intertwining of joy and sorrow as are flower and thorn. This image holds a special symbolism for a medieval woman such as Julian who would have been familiar with a wide variety of crowns and wreaths – for tournament victors, for brides, and also for religious women on the day of their consecration. These last garlands can vary from the silver 'mitra' to a flowered circlet or actual thorn-branch, each in its own way highlighting a different aspect of Christ's passion – its preciousness, its fecundity, its pain. For the disciple-soul, the joy of brideship must mature into a sharing of the passion; only then can it be transformed in the radiant joy of the

110

resurrection. 'To desire to share in the kingdom of our Spouse, Jesus Christ, and to enjoy it, and yet to be unwilling to have any part in his dishonours and trials is ridiculous',[7] writes Teresa in her pithy way. Julian does not merit any reproach on this score, so earnest is her longing for the 'wound of compassion'.

The garland is in fact the victory wreath of Jesus. Julian sees the reality underlying the outward form. He is 'his Majesty' despite appearances; the eye of faith discerns the Saviour in the 'Ecce Homo'.

After a brief introductory description, Julian digresses into exclamations of joy, wonder and humility, resuming her theme in ch. 7, and concentrating on the flowing blood which is hot, fresh, plentiful. Teresa's own favourite 'meditation picture' was the scourging at the pillar. Thérèse too was deeply moved at the sight of blood flowing from the Lord's wounded hand as depicted on a cheap print. It seems that blood actually *flowing* has a power for evoking a response that more static representations do not enjoy. It conjures up the *living* death, the life-giving, out-flowing nature of the Son of Man. And so, returning to the crowned head, Julian sees the garland burgeoning as it were with the flowers of red beads, abundant in their exceptional fruitfulness. In the vivid vignette that follows I see Julian the woman most of all. She tells us very little about herself directly, but here is a glimpse of her – no fine lady from Norwich Castle, but an ordinary béguine, a dedicated woman of the burgher class, eyeing the fish in the market and noting the myriad raindrops falling from the eaves of her plain dwelling:

The great drops of blood fell down from under the crown of thorns like pellets, as though they burst out at the veins. As it came out it was brownish red for the blood was very thick. As it spread it became bright red and when it reached the brows it vanished. Even so the bleeding lasted long enough for me to see and understand many things.

It was so lovely and lifelike that there is nothing to compare it with. It was as plentiful as the drops of water that fall from the eaves after a great shower of rain, that

111

fall so thick that no one can count them. And they were as round as the scale of a herring as they spread on the forehead.

These three things came into my mind at the time; pellets for roundness as the drops of blood come out; scales of herring as they spread on the forehead; drops from the eaves for the uncountable number.[8]

Where is there anywhere else in mystical literature such a powerful pictorial description from a sharp-eyed visionary? One who, we can well imagine, missed little in the natural world around her!

The profuse blood, red, fresh, living is part of a scene 'vivid and lifelike, hideous and dreadful, sweet and lovely'. In it seeming opposites are combined, for it shows many aspects of Jesus, who in his suffering is 'lowest and gentlest, most homely and most kind'. Here is a theme dear to both Julian and Teresa: Jesus, friend and companion, not *forcing* his way in but humbly asking for our human response. This is the heart of the eremitical vocation where friendship with and imitation of the poor, humble, suffering Christ go hand in hand.

From humanity to divinity

The wounded head and disfigured face of Jesus are symbolic of his whole person being poured out for us, given totally, drop by drop, yet he harbours no bitterness, is filled with a spirit of surrender. He is love made vulnerable, and from him, pierced and piteous, we are made privy to a deeper understanding of the Trinity, of God. Teresa, in the well-known ch. 22 of her *Life*, stresses that in her experience the *only* way we come to God is through the man Jesus. She writes:

> I can see clearly . . . that it is God's will, if we are to please him and he is to grant us great favours, that this should be done through his most sacred Humanity . . . Very, very many times have I learned this by experience: the Lord has told it to me. I have seen clearly that it is by this door

that we must enter if we wish his Sovereign Majesty to show us great secrets . . . That way alone is safe.[9]

And she continues by noting the lives of many saints who took this path. Julian, had Teresa known of her, would definitely be placed in this illustrious list. For Julian, when speaking of Jesus, says she includes always the whole Trinity (ch. 4); and she is right, for does not St Paul, one of those Teresa so generously lauds, state that 'in him dwells the fullness of the Godhead corporeally'? The passion of Christ takes us into the heart of the Trinity; through it we have a glimpse into the meaning of the words 'God is love' – this transcendent God who has been subject to time, this God who is our maker, keeper, eternal lover, our joy and happiness.

Everything that comes to us is a gift from one who is pure goodness. This is demonstrated supremely in the incarnation. Having given us his own Son, God can refuse us nothing else. There can be no grounds for doubting when we have received a proof such as this.

From gazing upon the Creator Julian 'sees' the sustaining sweetness of God interpenetrating the whole of creation which is summed up in Christ. Beside him all other things are tiny, insignificant, the size of a mere hazelnut. True, creation is held in being by love, but so small is the universe in comparison with its maker that no one could make the mistake of thinking this little thing worthy of the human heart with its infinite capacity. Those who realize the smallness of created things, and their inability to satisfy, cannot possibly rest in them as if they had value outside of God. It is madness to think that anything less than him is worthy of our entire devotion. And as Julian ponders this truth she speaks a prayer that can be used by all of us, for she sees that it gives God joy when 'a humble soul comes to him plainly, openly, simply'. A soul which wants God answers the desire of God to give himself fully to the soul; that, in itself, is a touch of the Spirit. To long for him is to possess him already in some mysterious way.

'God, of your goodness, give me yourself, for you are enough for me. There is nothing less I can ask that is

113

worthy of you, and if I ask for anything else I shall be always lacking. For only in you I have all.'[10]

From the divinity to our humanity
The joy inherent in the Trinity, fullness of life and love, leads Julian to a more profound comprehension of what that love means *for us*, and here she adopts the metaphor of clothing. We may imagine her prostrate on her bed in her darkened room, feeling herself to be at death's door and clad in a light shift. Perhaps in the background she hears the attendant priest reciting the penitential psalms, for she uses the exact words of Psalm 102 and could well apply the following verses to her condition:

> He has broken my strength in mid-course
> he has shortened the days of my life . . .
> Of old you laid the foundations of the earth,
> and the heavens are the work of your hands.
> They will perish, but you will endure;
> they will all wear out like a garment.
> You will change them like clothes that are changed
> But you are the same, and your years endless.
>
> (Ps.102:23–7)

This woman, prostrate with extreme weakness, knows herself to be upheld, enfolded lightly and warmly in the embrace of her maker, clothed in God's goodness in a manner that is unchanging. Although Julian uses the word *enfolded* there is no hint that this means some type of restriction. The enveloping of God is full of light, warmth, beauty, tenderness. Julian is clothed by God as of old he had clothed Israel his beloved bride (Isa. 61:10). It reminds us of St Paul in the New Testament exhorting his converts to be clothed with gentleness and compassion. These are garments which will never wear out, rather they become ever more radiant, and prepare the Church-bride for the heavenly nuptials (Rev. 19:7, 8; 21:2). The knowledge that we are clothed in the goodness of God makes the soul cleave to him as bride to beloved; she is 'mantled' together with him. It is *because* of God's love that we are not left naked, but protected. Our humanity is

114

in very truth a gift of his love, for it is made in his likeness and one'd to his Son. God's goodness is not all for himself; it is, rather, *all for us*. Once the soul understands this it is revitalized, drawn as by a magnet to its source: wholly loved, how can it not desire to be wholly loving in return?

Another way Julian recognizes the Creator's love is through the vision of the crucifix which enkindles joy. The face of the suffering Son is a proof of God's 'friendliness', and we must hold on to this in faith. The helplessness, the lowliness, of the crucified reveals the condescension of the Lord. He is totally like us in the flesh, with the same bodily needs. He has become out of love our equal and our comrade. By gazing upon the cross we develop a better sense of proportion. It is to him we must look if we are to understand ourselves aright and see life in its true light.

> Fix your eyes on the Crucified One [writes Teresa] and all will seem easy. If his Majesty proved his love for us by such stupendous labours and sufferings, how can you seek to please him by words alone?[11]

And lastly, God gives Julian the revelation of his goodness for *our* peace and comfort. She is his instrument, she 'sees' for those who walk in dark faith, and God has used her, not because *she* is good, but because *he* is. How similar to Teresa. Revelations are spurious if they inculcate pride in the recipient.

> There can be no question of our wanting or not wanting to see the vision. (This is God's work, not dependent on our volition.) It is clear that our Lord wants of us only humility and shame, our acceptance of what is given and our praise of the Giver.[12]

The point, I feel, is that were we *really* to believe in God's goodness and the gift he has made of his Son, it would be impossible to want anything 'extra'. Our flesh has been sanctified and redeemed *as it is*; this is a truth far more extraordinary than any passing psychic phenomena. All that another person can do is to point out to us what is already ours.

Corollary of the showing

What specially interests me is the conclusions Julian draws from her first revelation, and how they tie in exactly with Teresa's own advice to those who wish to follow the path of prayer to union with God. As I have already mentioned, at the beginning of her book *The Way of Perfection*, Teresa, after long years of experience, is asked to set down for her sisters the path to travel. She lists three things essential for interior and exterior peace, without which there can be no progress: detachment, love for one another, and true humility – this last named being the most important; and I see that Julian also points us along the same route.

Humility. The primary place Julian gives to humility seems to be exemplified in our blessed Lady who is 'brought to mind' as being very young. It is Mary who symbolizes the soul of each of us in relation to God – a child, with no self-importance. By surrendering herself to the love of God she is filled with wisdom, humility, reverent wonder. She knows the gulf between Creator and creature, and yet it is her *humility* which permits her to say a saving 'yes' to his plan of redemption. Teresa, in like manner, wants us to see that humility consists in this readiness to do all that the Lord may require of us. She writes:

> Reflect that true humility consists to a great extent in being ready for what the Lord desires to do with you and happy that he should do it, and always considering yourselves unworthy to be called his servants . . . I do not mean that it is for us to say what we shall do, but that we must do our best in everything, for the choice is not ours but God's.[13]

Humility therefore is learnt, as was Mary's, not from continually looking at self but at God. By fixing our eyes on Christ we are raised above cowardly and timid thoughts and enabled to say 'yes' to life.[14] Mary is the image of the beloved and loving soul who responds to her maker with utter trust, and we are summoned to a like surrender, for love and humility are intermingled; we cannot have one without the other.[15]

Would that, like Mary, we would allow God to love our 'littleness', care for us as he wants to, clothe us as he wants

116

to. But we, not being humble, are always struggling away, ashamed of our nakedness. To be one who 'turns round' towards God is to 'repent' in the real sense of trusting in the grace of God. Grace can do *anything*. The humble person conceives Christ anew and gives him once more to the world. Here is a wisdom that seems foolishness and yet bears abundant fruit.

Detachment. From the vision of creation's insignificance and smallness Julian is enabled to see the world in proper perspective – it just isn't worth making an end in itself of something so paltry. 'We need to know how small creation is, and to count all things that are made as nothing if we are to love and have God who is uncreated.' For the spiritual person, detachment means ultimately rest, peace, joy; without it we are not free to soar heavenwards 'unburdened by the leaden weight of earth'.[16] Detachment, however, is not something violent, nor an abuse of creation, nor a turning-one's-back on the things of this world – for how could we despise what God holds so tenderly in being? Detachment means rather setting our hearts on 'the world of lasting joys' – a phrase which frequently occurs in liturgical prayers, and which makes us masters, not slaves of created things.[17] In the true light of God, detachment is not so much a 'giving-up' as an awakening to the realization that the only thing ultimately worth having is God – all else pales by comparison. Genuine love is always giving, growing; false love wants to cling, to hoard, to keep. Detachment means a refusal to hold on to anything that keeps us from giving ourselves to God. This requires faith of course. It is so much easier and more reassuring to have things to rely on: 'His will is for us to desire the eternal, whereas we prefer that which passes away.'[18] Genuine mystical love always involves total detachment, otherwise we cannot be free; but once free we are enabled to love all 'with a more genuine love, a greater passion . . . And such souls are always much fonder of giving than of receiving, even in their relations with the Creator himself. This, I say, merits the name of love, which name has been usurped from it by those other base affections'.[19]

Love for others. We cannot love the Lord without including

love for others, for love is *one*. Real love springs from detachment and shows itself in practical ways. Besides this, on the
invisible level, prayer, solitude, 'seeing' are not meant for
an individual in isolation. Julian and Teresa are both very
conscious that they are part of the Church; and if they are
the objects of God's care so is everyone else, with whom they
are united by spiritual bonds 'in Christ'. As Julian says, God
made all, loves all, and whoever loves his fellow-Christians
for God's sake loves *all* that is. Nobody may separate herself
from the whole: there are no mystical heights which transcend
this basic obligation, and for Julian it is the source of her
greatest hope 'for I am united in love with my fellow-
Christians'. Teresa puts the same idea in her inimitable, very
practical way:

> We cannot know whether we love God although there may
> be strong reasons for thinking so, but there can be no doubt
> about whether we love our neighbour or no. Be sure that
> in proportion as you advance in fraternal charity you are
> increasing in your love of God.[20]

All that Julian and Teresa write is an attempt to share what
God has entrusted to them. There is no selfish hoarding, and
time and again they insist on not judging others, showing
care, tenderness, concern. Each seems to have been the
confidante of numerous people, yet there is no condemnation
of sinners. It is true that God enlarges hearts to a capacity
we seldom dream of, hearts which reflect his own compassion,
and Julian and Teresa possess such hearts. The only hard
words they have are for themselves; they do not notice the
plank in their brother's eye, but only the speck in their own!

So we can see that our two women draw from their extraordinary prayer-life what is pure commentary on the teachings of
the Gospel: we must become servants, little ones, trusting in
God, with the humble attitude of Mary who heard and did
the Lord's word. We must take up our cross daily, allowing
no other relationship or thing, however precious, to divert
our hearts from the Saviour, and we must love our neighbours
as he has loved them. This is a programme enough surely for

118

the most ambitious, yet so simple we can bypass it and think *real* religion consists in spectacular accomplishments and esoteric experiences, available only to a chosen few. No, *everything* is to be found in the Lord, crucified and risen, and to whom we have unhindered access in faith and in each other.

Julian and Teresa, after their visions, both adopted a way of life involving strict reclusion, but only so as to have, in God, wider, more all-embracing human sympathies. What they have been given is given to and for all of us. It is for our comfort and instruction.

These two practical women, gifted yes, but homely and devoted, are living examples for us of what it means to be the 'friend of Jesus' – that, with the help of God's grace, is what the Christian life is all about. It is a friendship growing ever deeper, ever more penetrating. We may not all have to retire to an actual cell, but the cell within is a 'must'. Like Julian and Teresa we must gaze upon the cross, the cross which has been marked on our foreheads at baptism and which needs to be engraved gradually upon our hearts. Neither woman has any desire to divorce herself from the life of the Church nor to place herself in any way above others. Each is very much a product of her time and culture, with similar leanings towards eremiticism and constant prayer. Each has grasped that in having God she has everything else, and the leap of faith which affirms this is borne out for her by personal experience – God alone suffices.

Julian	Teresa
God, of your goodness,	Nothing must disturb you
give me yourself,	nothing affright you.
for you are enough for me.	All things pass save God
There is nothing less I can ask	who does not change.
that is worthy of you,	Patience obtains all things.
and if I ask for anything else	He who has God
I shall be always lacking.	can want for nothing.
For only in you I have all.	*God alone suffices.*

119

Translations from Julian's *Revelations of Divine Love* are by Sheila Upjohn with two exceptions which are by Clifton Wolters (Harmondsworth 1966). Translations from *The Life of St Teresa of Jesus* are by David Lewis (1910), from *The Way of Perfection* by E. Allison Peers (1972), and from *The Interior Castle* by the Benedictines of Stanbrook (1912)

1 *RDL* ch. 7.
2 *Way of Perfection* ch. 4.
3 *Life* ch. 28.
4 *RDL* ch. 9.
5 *WP* ch. 18.
6 *Life* ch. 28.
7 *WP* ch. 13.
8 *RDL* ch. 7.
9 *Life* ch. 22.
10 *RDL* ch. 5.
11 *Interior Castle* Mans. 7.
12 *Life* ch. 29. (The remark in parenthesis is mine!)
13 *WP* ch. 17.
14 *IC* Mans. 1.
15 *WP* ch. 16.
16 *WP* ch. 10.
17 *WP* ch. 19.
18 *WP* ch. 42.
19 *WP* ch. 6.
20 *IC* Mans. 5.

Woman of Consolation and Strength

Robert Llewelyn

It has, I believe, been too seldom appreciated that the teaching of Julian that there is no wrath in God is quite basic to the theology of her *Revelations of Divine Love*. The doctrine is one of the pillars on which Julian's teaching rests and without it the main thrust of her book – 'the deep and wonderful knowledge of the constancy of God's love'[1] – could not be sustained. It is true that almost all the references to the doctrine are contained within a few chapters of one 'shewing' but in the writing of that showing (the fourteenth) Julian says:

> And my soul was led by love and drawn by strength to understand this *in every showing*. Our good Lord showed that it is so, and he showed, in truth, that it is so through his great goodness. And he wills that we should long to understand it – that is, in so far as created things can understand it.[2] (Italics mine here and below)

Apart from this showing the only other reference to the wrath of God comes briefly in the fifth showing where Julian writes, 'But in God there can be no anger as I see it'.[3] There is, it is true, reference to God's anger in the thirteenth showing but a careful reading of the passage will show that it is God's *supposed* anger to which Julian refers, that is to say, to the subjective sense of God's anger which we may experience in our sinning, an experience designed to lead us to repentance and amendment of life, so that 'God's wrath' (as we believe it to be) 'may be quenched'. The passage goes on to say how it is only after our restoration to God that it is given us to *see* that God's countenance was not changed towards us in our sin (though we might have 'seen' it earlier by faith) but that the nature of his love remained constant.[4]

Let us look more closely at Julian's teaching as contained in her fourteenth revelation:

> And so *in all these showings* it seemed to me that it was right and proper for us to see and know that we are sinners, and do many evil deeds we ought not to do, and leave many good deeds undone that we ought to do, and that we deserve to incur pain and anger because of this. And notwithstanding all this I saw truly that our Lord was never angry, nor never shall be, for he is God.[5]

> He is goodness, life, truth, love and peace. His love and his wholeness cannot allow him to be angry. For I saw truly that it is against the nature of his strength to be angry, and against the nature of his wisdom, and against the nature of his goodness. God is the goodness that knows no anger, for he is nothing but goodness. Our soul is joined to him – unchangeable goodness – and there is neither anger nor forgiveness between our soul and God, in his sight.[6]

> For, by the teaching I had beforehand, I understood that the mercy of God should be the forgiveness of his anger which our sins had caused. For I thought the anger of God was worse than any other pain for a soul whose intention and desire is to love. And so I thought the forgiveness of his anger should be one of the main points of his mercy. But in spite of everything that I longed to see – and did see – I could not see this *in all the showings*.[7]

> I saw no anger, except on man's part, and God forgives this anger in us. For anger is no more than a perversity and striving against peace and love. And it is caused either by lack of strength, or lack of wisdom, or lack of goodness. This lack is not found in God, but in us.[8]

> I needs must grant that the purpose of God's mercy and of his forgiveness is to lessen and quench our anger. For

122

this was a high marvel to the soul and it was shown continually *in all the showings*, and I looked on it carefully; it was shown that, of his nature, our Lord cannot forgive, for he cannot be angry. It would be impossible.[9]

It is absolutely impossible that God should be angry. For anger and friendship are two opposites. And so he who quenches and ends our anger must therefore be always loving, gentle and kind – which is the opposite of anger. For I saw full surely that wherever our Lord appears, peace reigns and anger has no place. For I saw no whit of anger in God – in short or in long term. For truly, as I see it, if God could be angry, even a little, we should never have life or place or being.[10]

And when, through the power of mercy and grace, we are made humble and gentle, we are wholly safe. Then suddenly the soul is at one with God, when it is truly at peace with itself, for no anger is found in him.[11]

Julian could hardly have made herself more plain. It will, however, have been seen that in rejecting the idea of wrath in God Julian does not eliminate the concept of wrath completely. But it is, she says, in us and not in God, and she describes it as 'a perversity and striving against peace and love'. Moreover, she tells us that the work of God's love, which is compassionate and never wrathful, is, as it meets us her 'even-Christians', 'to lessen and quench our anger'. This compassionate love is in no way dependent upon our spiritual state for, in her words, 'whether we are clean or foul it is all one to his love'.[12] Sufficient is it that we desire to receive God or that we pray that we may desire to receive him. Yet even if we do not receive him but reject him, not even that can change the unchanging nature of his love, though its effect on us (so long as we deliberately remain in that state) will be to increase the corruption within ourselves leading us not towards life but to spiritual death. As a loyal daughter of the Church Julian accepts her teaching on hell – uneasily one feels in regard to its everlastingness – and she balances her

belief with the conviction that at the last love shall be everywhere triumphant.

There are many informed Christians today who accept
Julian's teaching that there is no wrath in God. It is difficult,
however, to find evidence of that belief in the traditional
Church. One writer of distinction who went to great pains to
defend it was William Law, best known for his *Serious Call to
a Devout and Holy Life*, who has been regarded as the greatest
of the post-Reformation English mystics. I have written of his
presentation in what is often considered to be his greatest
work – *The Spirit of Love* – in a recent book *Love Bade Me
Welcome*[13] to which the interested reader may be referred.
Since its publication it has been brought to my notice that
Origen, philosopher and theologian of the third century, was
pointing his readers in the same direction. He writes:

> If you hear of God's anger and his wrath do not think of
> anger and wrath as emotions experienced by God . . . we,
> too, put on a severe face for children not because that is our
> true feeling but because we are accommodating ourselves to
> their level . . . if we let our kindly feelings towards the child
> show in our face and allow our affections for it to be clearly
> seen we spoil the child and make it worse. So God is said
> to be wrathful and declares he is angry in order that you
> may be corrected and improved.[14]

When recently I quoted those words on the radio my inter-
viewer exclaimed, 'Ah, it's just like me and my little dog!'
The same thought may have occurred to the reader. The little
dog suffered the experience of his mistress's anger and was
chastened and corrected thereby. But that was a subjective
experience only. Objectively and truthfully his mistress's
compassion still rested on him; perhaps, indeed, it was drawn
out yet more by the misdemeanour which occasioned her
rebuke. Every loving parent will know that it is so, too,
between them and their children, and it cannot be otherwise
between God and ourselves. Michael McLean helpfully
writes:

> There can be no anger in [God]. What we seem to experi-

ence as anger, what we call anger, is in fact completely in ourselves, and is simply a name to express the sensation caused in a sinner by the fire of God's love.[15]

Nor can it be other in regard to God and the souls in hell. It will seem to them that the anger of God rests upon them but that will be because their sin – their bitterness and malice and blindness – has twisted their moral vision. By contrast, as the angels, whose vision is clear and true, look upon God in relation to hell, it will be clear to them that his loving compassion rests upon these souls too, and that he would draw them also to himself by the cords of love, if only their now fixed stubbornness and irreversible blindness (to use traditional western concepts: the eastern Church – enhearten- ingly – keeps hope alive) did not prevent it. St Catherine of Genoa describes the love of God 'as *one* fire, experienced as hell, purgatory or love according to the spiritual state of the one plunged into it' (my italics).[16] It is the degree of 'wrath in ourselves' (to use Julian's term) which determines the manner in which we experience God's unchanging compassionate love. The danger is lest we accept our subjec- tive feeling as fact, instead of leaping beyond feeling, in the power of faith, to lay hold on the reality itself. It is through the manifestation of love on Calvary, so clearly reflected in Julian's writings, that we are enabled to do this.

It is no part of my purpose to question the limited value of a belief in a God who may be angry. It is true that the belief is sometimes expressed crudely and harmfully, but where it is propounded at its best God's love and his anger are seen as the opposite sides of one coin and in the final analysis God is always seen as working for our good. Yet, belief in a sometimes angry God should be seen as a relative truth only, conserving certain values as, for example, God's passionate care for our welfare, his holiness, abhorrence of evil, and the righteousness of his love. A truth which supports these concepts, though relative only, is not to be lightly discarded, and certainly not until we can move into the more absolute truth into which Julian's theology takes us. To discard one image before we are ready to take on another approximating more closely to the truth is as likely as not to leave us floundering in a spiritual vacuum. Yet Christian maturity demands, I believe, that at some stage we discard the image of tradition and adopt that which Julian supplies. It makes a tremendous difference to ourselves and others whether we accept it or not.

First, in regard to myself. If God is how Julian depicts him to be then in whatever state I now am I may never have the picture of an angry God standing over against me. There has, perhaps, been a fall from grace, a grievous fall perhaps, and once again I come to myself and turn to God to seek his help. If he is a sometimes wrathful God, then this my sin (in the words of *The Book of Common Prayer*) has 'provoked his wrath and indignation against [me]', and I shall be left wondering whether my expression of penitence and sorrow has been sufficient to enable him to change the aspect of his countenance towards me. But if God is such that his compassion rests upon me at all times, even in my sins, then the moment I turn to him I shall know that the work of restoration has already begun. The change is always to be on my part and not on God's. God's compassionate love is at all times flowing out to meet me, and nothing I can do can ever muddy the waters of the stream at its source. The fountain ever and again pours forth water pure and clear, unadulterated by any tinge of wrath. It is true that its effect upon me will depend upon the nature of my response but that is because of 'the wrath' within me which may be quenched or deepened, and not because of any wrathful disposition in God. Julian even goes so far as to say (when she is talking with strict theological accuracy) that God cannot forgive our sins, a startling thought at first, but what she means is that forgiveness would involve a change of God's attitude towards us and this can never be. She writes: '[When we pray, the soul is made] willing and responsive towards God. There is no kind of prayer which can make God more responsive to the soul, for God is always constant in love.'[17] Every renewed turning to God means simply that his forgiveness – already there – can become operative in ourselves. When we are open to receive it, forgiveness can be consummated.

Moreover, Julian's teaching is that our very falls, if they

ground us more surely in self-knowledge and help us towards
that truth about ourselves which is humility, are all taken up
into God's purpose, and in the end will be found instrumental
to the fullness of our salvation. She explains her meaning in
these words:

> And then he allows some of us to fall more severely and
> distressingly than before – at least that is how we see it.
> And then it seems to us, who are not always wise, that all
> we set our hands to is lost. But it is not so. We need to fall
> and we need to see that we have done so. For if we never
> fell we should not know how weak and pitiable we are in
> ourselves. Nor should we fully know the wonderful love of
> our maker. In heaven we shall see truly and everlastingly
> that we have grievously sinned in this life; notwithstanding,
> we shall see that this in no way diminished his love, nor
> made us less precious in his sight. The testing experience
> of falling will lead us to a deep and wonderful knowledge
> of the constancy of God's love which neither can nor will
> be broken because of sin. To understand this is of great
> profit.[18]

And a little later she writes: 'When we fall he holds us
lovingly, and graciously and swiftly raises us.'[19]

But, as always, there is balance in Julian. Just as St Paul
feared that his preaching of the unlimited grace of God might
cause some to say, 'if this be so, let us sin that grace may
abound', so Julian warns us against presuming on the
exceeding generosity of God's love.

> But, then, because of all this spiritual comfort that has
> been promised, a man or woman might be led through
> folly, to say or think: 'If this is true then it is good to sin
> so as to get a better reward', or else to think sin less sinful.
> Beware of this thinking, for truly if this thought comes it
> is untrue, and comes from the enemy of that true love that
> shows us all this comfort. This same blessed love teaches
> us that we should hate sin simply for the sake of love. And
> I am sure, by what I feel myself, that the more every loving
> soul sees of this, in the courteous love of our Lord God,

the less he wants to sin and the more he is ashamed . . . For sin is so vile and so greatly to be hated that it can be likened to no other pain except the pain of sin. And I was shown no harder hell than sin, for there is no hell but sin for a loving soul.[20]

But we may be affected in another way by Julian's teaching of an all compassionate God in whom no wrath is found. I have written on this elsewhere and the passage may be quoted here:

Largely through the writings of C. G. Jung, we have become aware of a shadow side of ourselves standing for the darker element of our nature which it is difficult for us to acknowledge even to ourselves. It is, consequently, easy for us to reject or disown this part of us; whereas we have to accept it and allow it to offer up to the whole person whatever is good within it that it may be integrated with the conscious life, making for a fuller and more complete man or woman in Christ. The Christian who believes in a God capable of wrath will believe that here in the darker area of his life God's wrath will find the material on which it may be supremely exercised. Hence, in so far as he is a God-fearing and conscientious person he will tend to shut down the lid tightly on it. If, however, there be no wrath in God, but only a loving compassion, he will not be fearful to face this area in the power of the Holy Spirit and allow it to be exposed. The way is thus open for integration and healing to take place. I believe it to be true that if ever we are to grow into full maturity in Christ, it is essential that we eventually come to believe that there is no wrath in God. I would add that we are to let the Holy Spirit take us to that point in his own time. To believe the right thing at the wrong time is (for the person concerned) to believe the wrong thing.[21]

It may at this point be of interest to reflect that the revisers of *The Book of Common Prayer* have, in the *Alternative Service Book* (ASB) of 1980, eliminated all references to the wrath of God.

It makes a great difference, too, in our attitude towards one another whether we believe Julian's teaching at this point or not. Julian writes that we are 'to be like [God] in wholeness of endless love . . . towards our fellow-Christians',[22] and that must, of course, mean that towards others we reflect God's compassionate love. 'All compassion to one's fellow-Christians, exercised in love', she tells us, 'is a mark of Christ's indwelling.'[23] And in another place:

> The soul which would remain at peace when another's sin comes to mind, must fly as from the pains of hell, asking for God's protection and help. Looking at another's sin clouds the eyes of the soul, hiding for the time-being the fair beauty of God – unless we look upon this sinner with contrition with him, compassion on him, and a holy longing to God for him. Otherwise it must harm and disquiet the soul that looks on these sins.[24]

Our love for one another must necessarily follow the same pattern as God's love for ourselves, a pattern in which, as we have seen, forgiveness *precedes* repentance and does not simply follow upon it, even though we know that the *appropriation* of forgiveness must await our renewed turning to God. Christian ethic follows directly from Christian theology, and a sub-Christian theology – as (it is maintained) is one which acknowledges wrath in God – must lead to a corresponding modification of our attitudes towards one another. The direct link between the two – the nature of God's love for us and of our love for one another – is unmistakably set before us in the words of Jesus: 'Love your enemies and pray for your persecutors, only so can you be children of your heavenly Father, who makes his sun to rise on the good and bad alike, and sends the rain on the honest and the dishonest' (Matt. 5:44–5). It is impossible for a man to pray for his 'enemies' while he is willingly harbouring anger against them. Reflection on this fact alone must of itself yield an insight into the 'wrathlessness' of God as portrayed by Julian.

Two powerful quotations may be invoked to emphasize our point. Metropolitan Anthony Bloom writes:

One should not expect to be forgiven because one has changed for the better; neither should one make such a change a condition for forgiving other people; it is only because one is forgiven, one is loved, that one can begin to change, not the other way round. And this we should never forget, though we always do.[25]

And Dorothy Sayers writes crisply: 'while God does not, and man dare not, demand repentance as a condition for *bestowing* pardon, repentance remains an essential condition for *receiving* it.'[26]

This article is being written at the end of a week in which, along with the heroism, comradeship and sacrifice which war evokes, we are reminded of the nature of the tyranny against which we fought. It will not have passed unnoticed amongst lovers of Julian that 8 May, marking the end of hostilities in Europe, is, too, her festival day, the anniversary of her visions of God's love. Julian is the apostle of reconciliation, her wisdom and sanity transcending all national and denominational boundaries, and the strong and enduring love she holds out in the name of the crucified and risen Christ is the only balm which may heal our wounds. It is, of course, right that we may never forget, just as we may never forget the no lesser evil of the crucifixion of Jesus – God himself made man and we nailed him to a cross. There it stands, and must ever stand, on the pages of history for all to see. But we are to forget in the sense that we no longer hold the remembrance of the scene *against* those who laid him bare, and this sort of forgetting is what we mean by forgiveness. Or, to put it in other words, God does not require us to forget – forgetting is in fact an impossibility where any event affects us deeply (can any forget a wartime bereavement?) – but God does require us to forgive and by his grace we are enabled to do so. It is not for us to sit in judgement upon any man, and in any case by what measuring line do we measure the extent of another's sin against that of our own? It may be that the hearts of some are still hardened, and that they cannot receive the forgiveness which God or man is offering to them. No matter, the spirit of forgiveness must continue to flow. I recall reading how in a recent hunger strike, food was brought to the strikers every day. It was left untouched but the offer was not withdrawn. It is so between God and man in relation to the forgiveness of our sins.

To remember a person's sin against him is in fact to impute blame. Perhaps we can see this best in relation to ourselves. To remember our sins (in the sense of being able to remember them if we wish) is psychologically speaking healthy, to remember them against ourselves is not. This means that we have not forgiven ourselves, or to put it otherwise that we are blaming ourselves. The moment we stop blaming ourselves, at that very instant we begin to forgive. So, too, the forgiveness of another is to cease from blame. Julian insists a number of times that God does not blame us for our sins. The thought puzzled her because it conflicted with what she had been taught by the Church:

> For I know by the daily teaching of Holy Church, and by my own feelings, that the blame for our sin hangs heavily upon us, from the first man until the time we come up to heaven. This, then, was my wonder – that I saw our Lord putting no more blame upon us than if we were as clean and holy as the angels in heaven.[27]

And at another point Julian writes: 'The Lord looks on his servant with pity and not with blame.'[28]

Where God forgives he imputes no blame, and the test of our own forgiveness, whether towards ourselves or another, is whether we no longer attribute blame to the one concerned. Ask whether you still blame another for an offence and you will know whether you have truly forgiven him. It is easy to deceive ourselves here, to say in the secret place of the heart, 'I blame you for this but I have forgiven you'. In this way we secretly cling to a position of moral superiority over the other. We are up here, and he or she, the 'forgiven' one, is below us. This is not the forgiveness of the children of God. It is a part of the deep insight of Julian that she sees this so clearly. It is an application of the command of Jesus not to judge one another. It is true that in the kingdom of the world we must judge one another and we need our law courts and tribunals and the like if society is to be held together. But the laws of the kingdom of heaven are not as those of the world. Jesus gives us the parable of the labourers in the vineyard at the end of which all – independently of their hours of work – are paid one 'penny'. It is an impossible concept in the economics of the world but true of the kingdom of heaven where love, without despising justice, transcends it. Hence the familiar phrase with which parables are introduced, 'The kingdom of heaven is likened to . . .'.

The forgiveness which imputes no blame is magnificently illustrated in the words of a Russian bishop as he went to his death:

> There will come a day when the martyr will be able to stand before the throne of God in defence of his persecutors and say, 'Lord I have forgiven in your name and by your example. You have no more claim against them any more'.

It is a filling up of the sufferings of Christ (Col. 1:24), a human echo of what Julian has said in ch. 51 of her *Revelations* where, relating the parable of the lord and the servant, she writes:

> And so has our good Lord Jesus taken upon him all our blame, and therefore our Father may not, does not wish to assign more blame to us than to his own beloved Son Jesus Christ.

Yet there is here in Julian a common-sense compromise, a concession to our state of imperfection. And so she writes:

> He says, 'Do not blame yourself too much, thinking that your trouble and distress is all your fault. For it is not my will that you should be unduly sad and despondent.' Our enemy tries to depress us by false fears which he proposes. His intention is to make us so weary and dejected, that we let the blessed sight of our everlasting friend slip from our minds.[29]

Not to blame ourselves briefly when we have done wrong would be slowly to erode any sense of responsibility for our actions. It is where blame lingers on, it may be for days and not infrequently for many years, that we become maimed people and growth in Christ is severely inhibited. St Paul's injunction that we do not let the sun go down upon our wrath makes a good guideline here. And yet it is a mark of the saints – and a witness to their humility – that after a fall they at once turn again in loving confidence to God with some reflection as, 'This, Lord, you know to be like me and apart from your grace I shall fall many times', and then go on their way without more ado. That is how it may be one day; meanwhile we must take ourselves as we are. And so to her 'even-Christians' Julian says, 'Do not blame yourself too much . . .'. And in another place she writes:

> And when we have fallen through frailty or blindness . . . he wills that we should see our wretchedness and humbly acknowledge it. But it is not his will that we should stay like this, nor does he will that we should busy ourselves with too much self-accusation; nor is it his will that we should despise ourselves. But he wills that we should quickly turn to him.[30]

It is in the last sentence that Julian would have us find the remedy for all our troubles, of which not the least for some temperaments is inordinate self-blame undermining strength and joy and making the soul weak and listless and near to despair. The remedy, Julian tells us, is prayer: 'When the soul is tempest-tossed, troubled and cut off by worries, then is the time to pray, so as to make the soul willing and responsive towards God.'[31]

Of Julian's own prayers we know little. They would almost certainly have been to some extent governed by the Ancrene Rule, a manual drawn up for solitaries a hundred years and more before her day. In the Shorter Text she gives evidence of her use of the 'Our Father, Hail Mary, and I Believe',[32] prayers which would have formed part of her daily Office. We may note that they are, too, the prayers of the rosary with which she would have been familiar.[33] The Ancrene Rule also provided a form of repetitive prayer bearing a marked affinity with that of the Jesus Prayer of the Orthodox Church. 'Jesus Christ, Son of the Living God, have mercy on us! Thou who didst condescend to be born of a virgin, have mercy on us!' The words were to be said continuously during dressing and frequently at other times. 'Have these words much in use, and in your mouth, as often as ye may, sitting and standing.'[34] And so in some such way the trial – and here we are speaking of chronic self-blame – becomes the instrument of our turning to God, and the whole process is set in motion by which, in Julian's words, our wounds shall be seen by God 'not as scars but as honours'. It is true that the trial may continue to be *felt* for some while. The important thing is that the will is now operating Godwards and in the end the feelings will fall into correspondence with the action of the will.

Elsewhere in this book Julian has been eloquently proclaimed as a woman of hope. One sphere in which we need to recapture this quality is where it relates to God's power to raise us up, no matter how far we have fallen; and, in Julian's thought, not only to raise us but to make our very sins the instruments of glory. Julian's words are here arresting in their boldness.

God showed that sin shall not be a shame to man, but a glory. For just as every sin brings its own suffering by truth, so every soul that sins earns a blessing by love . . . In this showing my understanding was lifted up to heaven. And then God brought happily to my mind David and others without number from the Old Law, and in the New Law he brought to my mind first Mary Magdalene, Peter and Paul, and those of India, and St John of Beverley – and also others without number. And he shows how the Church on earth knows of them and their sins, and it is no shame to them, but it is all turned to their glory.[35]

For the man or woman untouched by grace this must be one of Julian's hardest passages – an offence and stumbling-block. How can David's sin (how can my sin?) whereby he arranged with his general Joab for Uriah to be killed in battle that he might marry Bathsheba, his widow, be seen not as shame but as the forerunner of glory? Julian's answer comes later in the chapter after considering the fall of St John of Beverley, a saint on whom she looks in deep tenderness and

134

affection. She would have us know that no fall is to be seen ultimately as loss if it leads to contrition and a deepening knowledge of God's mercy, whereby pride and self-will can be overthrown, and our grounding in humility be made complete. And so it is she can write:

> God allowed him [St John of Beverley] to fall. But he mercifully upheld him so that he did not perish or lose time. And afterwards God lifted him up to much more grace. Because of the contrition and humility he had in this life, God has given him many joys in heaven, which go beyond those he would have had if he had not fallen.[36]

Earlier in the same chapter Julian has explained:

> Just as many sins are punished with much suffering because they are so bad, even so they shall be rewarded with many joys in heaven because of the suffering and sorrow they have caused the soul here on earth.[37]

Punished, in the sense of chastening, but:

> It is a beautiful humility – brought about by the grace and mercy of the Holy Spirit – when a sinful soul willingly and gladly accepts the chastisement our Lord himself would give us. It will seem light and easy, if only we will accept contentedly what he calls upon us to bear.[38]

We are not to forget that although the element of the wrath of God finds no place in Julian that of chastisement is everywhere assumed. But chastisement is to be seen never as the wrath which would oppose us but as the love which would draw and enable us. We find this note of God's chastening love introduced into the most tender part of Julian's writings where she is likening Christ's love to that of a mother's care for her child:

> A kind, loving mother, who knows and understands the needs of her child, looks after it tenderly as is her way and nature. And as it grows bigger she changes her ways but not her love. And when it grows older still she allows it to be punished, to break it from vice and lead it to goodness

and grace. And our Lord does the same thing in the same way, truly and well, to those he brings up.[39]

The varied relationship of God with his children is movingly described by Brant Pelphrey in his rewarding study *Love Was His. Meaning:*

> [Julian] sees that we relate to our heavenly father sometimes as little children, who need punishment and chiding; sometimes as helpless children who need rescuing; sometimes as wrathful children, who are nevertheless loved though we refuse love; and sometimes as mature children, or even as a beloved wife, who can return love as it is given. Underlying her concept of growth in the Holy Spirit, which is our growth in divine love, is a remarkable idea which needs to be heard today: that only love compels love in others, and creates maturity.[40]

God may even rejoice in our sorrow – albeit his rejoicing is tempered with compassion and pity – because he can see what is so often hidden from us, the splendour of the work which is being achieved. Thus:

> I saw so much, that I understood that our Lord, in his pity and compassion, can be pleased by his servant's tribulation. He lays upon everyone he longs to bring into his bliss something which is no blame in his sight, but for which they are blamed and despised in this world – scorned, mocked and cast out. He does this to offset the harm they should otherwise have from the pomp and vainglory of this earthly life, and to make their road to him easier, and to bring them higher in his joy without end. For he says, 'I shall shatter all your vain affections and your vicious pride, and after that I shall gather you up and make you kind and gentle, clean and holy by joining you to me.'[41]

Earlier in the same chaper Julian has foreseen that 'God's servants, Holy Church, shall be shaken in sorrow and anguish and tribulation in this world, as a cloth is shaken in the wind'. Yet it remains her conviction that love shall at the last be everywhere triumphant. The great words which have been given her that 'All shall be well, and all shall be well, and all manner of thing shall be well',[42] repeated several times in her writings, remain as her underlying assurance informing and sustaining all she has to say. God is, and ever has been, and ever will be most surely in control. He can (as St Augustine has put it) permit evil only so far as he is capable of transforming it into good. It is in that spirit that Julian can write:

> All that our Lord does is right, and all that he allows is praiseworthy ... Everything that is good is done by our Lord, and everything that is evil is done under his sufferance. I do not say that evil is praiseworthy but that our Lord's allowing it is praiseworthy. In this his goodness shall be known for ever by his loving-kindness and by the power of his mercy and grace.[43]

And a little earlier she has said, and it must be our closing thought:

> I saw in truth that God does all things, however small they may be. And I saw that nothing happens by chance but by the far-sighted wisdom of God. If it seems like chance to us it is because we are blind and blinkered. The things planned before the world began come upon us suddenly, so that in our blindness we say that they are chance. But God knows better. Constantly and lovingly he brings all that happens to its best end.[44]

I am gratefully indebted to Sheila Upjohn for all Julian quotations which, with one exception, are taken from *Enfolded in Love* (*EIL*) or *In Love Enclosed* (*ILE*) being 'Daily Readings with Julian of Norwich' and 'More Daily Readings with Julian of Norwich' (London 1980 and 1985 respectively). The page number is followed by the chapter number from *Revelations of Divine Love* (*RDL*).

1 *EIL* p. 37, *RDL* ch. 61.
2 *ILE* p. 51, *RDL* ch. 46.
3 *ILE* p. 17, *RDL* ch. 13.
4 *ILE* p. 44, *RDL* ch. 40.
5 *ILE* p. 50, *RDL* ch. 46.

6 *ILE* p. 51, *RDL* ch. 46.

7 *ILE* p. 52, *RDL* ch. 47.

8 *ILE* p. 53, *RDL* ch. 48.

9 *ILE* pp. 55–6, *RDL* ch. 48–9.

10 *ILE* p. 56, *RDL* ch. 49.

11 *ILE* p. 59, *RDL* ch. 49.

12 *EIL* p. 48, *RDL* ch. 76.

13 Robert Llewelyn, *Love Bade Me Welcome* (London and New York 1984), pp. 19, 36.

14 Origen, *Homilies on Jeremiah* 18.

15 *ILE* p. xiii, introduction by Michael McLean.

16 *Fairacres Chronicle* (spring 1985), p. 34.

17 *ILE* p. 49, *RDL* ch. 43.

18 *EIL* p. 37, *RDL* ch. 61.

19 *EIL* p. 38, *RDL* ch. 61.

20 *ILE* p. 46, *RDL* ch. 40.

21 *Love Bade Me Welcome*, pp. 24–5.

22 *ILE* p. 47, *RDL* ch. 30.

23 *EIL* p. 47, *RDL* ch. 28.

24 *EIL* p. 47, *RDL* ch. 76.

25 Metropolitan Anthony of Sourozh MD, DD, *Meditations on a Theme* (London 1971).

26 Dorothy Sayers, *Unpopular Opinions: twenty-one essays* (London 1951).

27 *ILE* p. 60, *RDL* ch. 50.

28 *EIL* p. 53, *RDL* ch. 82.

29 *EIL* p. 49, *RDL* ch. 77, 76.

30 *EIL* p. 52, *RDL* ch. 79.

31 *ILE* p. 49, *RDL* ch. 43.

32 See ch. 19 of the Shorter Text. The full sentence reads: 'For this we say the Our Father, Hail Mary, I Believe, with such devotion as God will give us.' Julian makes it clear that she used the prayers with intercessory intent.

33 The only mention of the rosary ('the telling of the beads.') in the *Revelations* is to its wrong use, 'aloud, with the mouth only, without the devotion, attention, and due care which we owe to God when we say our prayers'. See *RDL* ch. 69, trans. by Clifton Wolters (Harmondsworth 1966).

34 James Morton, *The Nun's Rule Being the Ancrene Rule Modernized* (Alexander Moring 1905), p. 13.

35 *ILE* p. 39, *RDL* ch. 38.

36 *ILE* p. 40, *RDL* ch. 38. The reference to St John of Beverley may supply internal evidence for the date of Julian's visions. The date is usually taken to be 8 May 1373 but it has been questioned whether the manuscript reading is VIII or XIII. St John of Beverley might have been especially in Julian's mind on 8 May since his festival fell on the

previous day. It is a pointer only and its signficance will be variously assessed.

37 *ILE* p. 39, *RDL* ch. 38.
38 *EIL* p. 49, *RDL* ch. 77.
39 *RDL* ch. 60 (the passage is not in *EIL* or *ILE*).
40 Brant Pelphrey, *Love Was His Meaning: the theology and mysticism of Julian of Norwich* (Salzburg 1982).
41 *ILE* p. 31, *RDL* ch. 28.
42 *ILE* pp. 29, 30, 34, 36, *RDL* chs. 27, 32.
43 *EIL* p. 14, *RDL* ch. 35.
44 *EIL* p. 12, *RDL* ch. 11.

Julian: Biographical Note

Of Julian's life little is known apart from scant details given in her book, some deductions which can be made, and a few pieces of external evidence in Norwich archives and *The Book of Margery Kempe.*

The following list indicates a *possible* chronology.

1342	Born – possibly in Norwich
c. 1360	Her prayer for three graces from God
1373, 8/9 May	Her Showings at the end of a week's illness
c. 1375	Entry into Cell at St Julian's Church
	Composition of the Short Text
1393	Composition of the Long Text
1413	Visit of Margery Kempe
c. 1420	Death (some place her death as late as 1429)

Of Julian's family we know nothing and even her name was probably taken from that of the church which in her day was already four hundred years old. She may have had some connection with the Benedictine nuns at Carrow Abbey (who had the right of presentation of the Vicars of St Julian's and control of the Cell) and may, possibly, have received some education there. It is unlikely she was a nun. She may well have lived according to the Rule for Anchoresses when she embraced the solitary life at St Julian's.

Julian was the first woman to write a book in the English language. There are three major versions of the Long Text, the earliest being a seventeenth-century copy, and one version of the Short Text of c. 1450 copying a lost manuscript of 1413. There are extracts in other archives. The first influential

141

translation, by Grace Warrack, was in 1901, and there have been numerous versions since.

Select Bibliography

The following texts are recommended:

Julian of Norwich: Showings, edited and translated by Edmund Colledge OSA and James Walsh SJ (Western Classics of Spirituality series, London, SPCK and New York, Paulist Press, 1978). Short and Long Text.

Julian of Norwich: Revelations of Divine Love, edited and translated by Clifton Wolters (Harmondsworth, Penguin Classics, 1966). Long Text only.

A Shewing of God's Love, edited and translated by Anna Maria Reynolds CP (London, Sheed and Ward, 1974). Short Text only.

Julian of Norwich. A Revelation of Love, edited by Marion Glasscoe. (Exeter, University of Exeter, 1976). Middle English Text only.

Enfolded in Love and *In Love Enclosed* (London, Darton Longman and Todd, 1980 and 1985 respectively). Each book, prepared and translated at the Julian Shrine, gives sixty daily readings from the Long Text.

For general reading:

At an advanced level: *Love Was His Meaning: the theology and mysticism of Julian of Norwich*, Brant Pelphrey (Salzburg Studies in English Literature, Institut für Anglistik und Amerikanistik, University of Salzburg, Salzburg, 1982). The book is in English; the quotations from Julian are in Middle English. The most comprehensive book on Julian to date.

At a popular level: *With Pity not with Blame*, Robert Llewelyn (London, Darton, Longman and Todd, 1982; New York, Paulist Press, 1985 under the title *All Shall Be Well*).

At an introductory level: *Who was Julian? A Beginner's Guide*, Michael McLean. Obtainable from the Julian Shrine, c/o All Hallows, Rouen Road, Norwich NR1 1QT at 75p post free.